Investigating the JUDG- MENT

To order additional copies of *Investigating the Judgment,* by John T. Anderson, call 1-800-765-6955.

Visit us at **www.reviewandherald.com** for information on other Review and Herald® products.

Investigating the JUDGMENT

Patterns of Divine Judgment

John T. Anderson

REVIEW AND HERALD® PUBLISHING ASSOCIATION
HAGERSTOWN, MD 21740

This book was
Edited by Gerald Wheeler
Copyedited by Jan Schleifer and James Cavil
Designed by GenesisDesign
Electronic makeup by Shirley M. Bolivar
Typeset: 10/14 Bookman

PRINTED IN U.S.A.

07 06 05 04 03   5 4 3 2 1

R&H Cataloging Service
Anderson, John Thomas, 1949-
    Investigating the judgment

        1. Judgment (Theology).   I. Title.

                    236.9

ISBN 0-8280-1736-0

Thanks

Chuck, Carl, Marvin, Mike, and Ben
for your special contributions to this project!

Contents

The Flood and the Investigative Judgment
The Tower of Babel and the Investigative Judgment
Sodom and Gomorrah and the Investigative Judgment
Joseph and the Investigative Judgment
The Passover and the Investigative Judgment
The Fall of Jerusalem and the Investigative Judgment
The Fall of Babylon and the Investigative Judgment
The Woman Taken in Adultery and the Investigative Judgment
The Second Fall of Jerusalem and the Investigative Judgment
Narrative Study Summary

Preface

I was sitting at my desk in the church office one day when one of our members walked in, and I asked him, "What time is it?" He gave me the correct time and then inquired where my watch was. I explained that there was nothing wrong with the watch, but that the strap had broken and I hadn't had a chance as yet to get another.

"Here, take mine," he offered.

"Oh no," I responded, "I'll be fine. It'll just be a day or two till I get my strap fixed, and I'll be OK until then."

"No," he insisted, "I want you to have my watch. Please, take it."

Again I tried to decline, repeating that it was just the strap that needed repair and that I'd have it back on my wrist in no time. But he was not to be refused!

"You don't understand. I'm giving you my watch. I want you to have it." At last I gave in, took the watch, and put it on, thanking him repeatedly. It didn't have the kind of band I was used to, and I felt a little awkward as I wore it that day, and so as I had intended, I purchased and installed a new strap. My trusty Timex was ticking away on my wrist in short order. The gift watch went into a drawer in my desk at home and stayed there.

Eventually I received an invitation to be the pastor of one of our churches in another area, and we moved away. Still the gift watch sat in the same drawer in my desk, now parked in our new home. Years passed. One Sunday morning my wife and I were reading the paper, and my eyes fell on some advertisements for watches. I commented on the pretty lofty prices some of them had. "I can't believe it. Some of these watches are $5,000; some even as much as $10,000. Why would anyone pay that much for a wristwatch?" I said, thinking fondly of my faithful $20 timepiece.

Without looking up, her attention glued to another section of the paper, she asked, "What kind of watches are those?"

Examining the ad, I replied, "They're Rolexes. They have a

crown on the face." Suddenly my mouth went dry and the color drained from my face. Jumping up from the couch, I sprinted to the other room. Jerking open the desk drawer, I pawed for the gift watch, which had been hibernating now for five or six years. Sure enough, to my utter astonishment there was the trademark crown and the name—Rolex.

Imagine my thoughts! My church member had presented me with his Rolex! Had my expressions of appreciation measured up to his generosity? What must he have thought as the next time he saw me I had the Timex back on and never wore the Rolex again? I walked slowly back to living room, the gift watch in hand, and said quietly to my wife, "You're never going to believe it. You remember the watch that our church member gave me that day when the strap broke on mine? It's a Rolex!"

I've had years to reflect on that experience and question how it was possible to receive such a gift and not know its true value (I did look at it and check the time a couple of times that first day, but still didn't recognize it for what it was!). It serves as an illustration for my feelings and convictions regarding the topic of study I share with you now.

A little more than 20 years ago I was in my garage, which at that time was doing double duty as a wood shop, making some dining room chairs. I remember the scene well: the stacks of partially assembled legs and supports, the crowded space, with tools and worktable barely leaving room to park the car (a compact at that), and the smell of mahogany sawdust in the air. Someone had given me a cassette tape to listen to, and since my hands and eyes, but not my ears, were engaged in the woodworking project, I set up the cassette player and clicked it on. The tape was a presentation by a former teacher at Pacific Union College, subsequent to the time when I was a student there, who expressed his lack of confidence in the church's position on the investigative judgment. Since he had not only been a pastor and teacher but had also authored a commentary on the book of Daniel, his testimony carried some weight.

His views challenged the thinking of many in the church, including me. As I look back on the past 20 years, I consider that tape to have been a blessing to me, in that it provoked me to study the subject of the investigative judgment as I had not done before—and might never have done. The result was that my study not only strengthened my confidence in the interpretation of Daniel 8:14 as understood by our pioneers, but brought new perspectives and impressions about God and His ways that I seriously doubt I would have gained had I not engaged in that study.

It was as if I had a cherished heirloom that I believed was plated in gold, only to have someone charge that it was not wrapped in real gold but iron pyrite, fool's gold. Then, prodded to have it appraised, I found to my delight that it was in actuality solid gold, not merely gold plate, and thus worth much more than I had originally suspected. Or, thinking back on my watch experience, upon closer examination the gift turned out to be a Rolex! My admiration for the historic Seventh-day Adventist position on the investigative judgment has grown immeasurably through this study.

May I take this opportunity to express my appreciation to you, reader, for joining me on this excursion and allowing me to point out to you those things that have impressed me. It is my intention that the journey be informative, interesting, and profitable. As with many trips, understanding increases if the traveler knows where the journey is leading, so before we start, I would like to share with you its goal and some of the scenic turnouts along the way. The final destination is a deeper appreciation of the character of the God who judges and a better grasp of that part of the judgment that precedes Jesus' return.

As we progress toward our final destination, after some foundational remarks we'll first take a look at a few prophecies in the Bible and see that the Scriptures do indeed present an aspect of the judgment that concludes before the Advent. Second, we'll focus on the word translated "cleansed" in the King James Version (KJV) of Daniel 8:14, and see that such a translation is not illegitimate and that the word has a powerful legal flavor. It has a courtroom atmosphere about it. The appearance of that word alone suggests judgment. Third, we'll examine a number of stories in the Bible that clearly portray a God who investigates before He takes action. At the very end we'll take a short look at Daniel 8:14 as being the answer to a question posed in the previous verse. Also we'll spend a moment examining a challenge raised by those who oppose the idea that Christ did not enter the Most Holy Place until 1844, since Scripture pictures Him at the right hand of the Father subsequent to His resurrection.

If at times our expedition seems to move at a little slower pace than at others, it is only because we need to pause to take a closer look at something important. Occasionally we may indulge a brief detour if it appears that the view we gain is justified and doesn't appreciably take us away from our main objective.

May I suggest that you approach the journey with a Bible in hand and a prayer in your heart. If you've always believed in the investigative judgment, I trust this study will confirm your faith. Perhaps you have a few doubts and questions about the subject. I hope this book will stimulate and challenge your thinking. Should you have concluded that the Bible does not support the teaching, I respectfully ask you to take another look. Or if you've never so much as heard about a pre-Advent judgment, it is my prayer that you will approach this study with an open mind. To all who join me on this journey, I invite you to take the time to study the passages to see whether these things be so. And above all, ask God to reveal Himself to you through His Word!

Introduction

I t's been more than a century and a half now since pulpits
across America and many other parts of the world thundered
the preaching of William Miller and his Advent disciples as they
proclaimed that Christ was going to return to the earth on October
22, 1844. Miller based his message largely on his understanding
of Daniel 8:14: "Unto two thousand and three hundred days; then
shall the sanctuary be cleansed" (KJV).

His study led him to believe that the "sanctuary" was this
earth, which the coming of Christ would "cleanse" by fire.
Believing, further, that a day in symbolic prophecy stood for a literal year, and that 457 B.C. was the date that instigated the ticking of the prophetic time clock, he concluded that our world would
come to a final and fiery end in 1844.

All of this reached an evangelistic crescendo in the fall of 1844.
Huge crowds, often numbering upward of 10,000, pressed together under canvas tents to hear the preaching of Miller, Joshua
V. Himes, Josiah Litch, Charles Fitch, and others whose message
was "Behold, the Bridegroom cometh." Through prophetic charts
and periodicals they expounded on the prophecies and brought
the Scriptures to life. Expectancy was in the air as people lived in
eager anticipation of soon meeting their Lord in the sky.

But by the dawn of October 23 a thick blanket of gloom and
depression had settled over those who just one day before thought
they would now be forever free of this world's woes and would be
winging their way to heaven. Many of Miller's adherents relin-
quished their faith and went back to their farms and jobs. Others
continued to set later dates, thinking the error had been with the
math in the prophetic equation.

A few of the former Millerites began to champion another
proposition, as Hiram Edson explained the view he received on
October 23 while crossing a field. Something monumental indeed

had happened at the conclusion of this longest of all time prophecies, but it was not the cherished event they had assumed. Christ was not coming to the earth in 1844, but had instead entered the Most Holy Place of the sanctuary in heaven to begin an investigative phase of judgment that must conclude prior to His return. Those who believed this position became the nucleus of what would later organize as the Seventh-day Adventist Church.

From the very first time this view was made public, the teaching of the investigative judgment has elicited criticism. The reinterpretation of Daniel 8:14, from William Miller's "Christ is coming back to this earth" to Hiram Edson's "Christ has entered the Most Holy," brought an immediate outcry from the theological community, some calling it "the greatest face-saving device in ecclesiastical history." Throughout the ensuing years the concept has drawn fire from objectors, our current age being no different. Most often the grenades have come from those outside the Seventh-day Adventist denomination, but at times shells have exploded from within, sometimes triggered by those whom many had placed confidence in as being stalwart Adventists. These detonations have shaken the faith of many members of the church, including not a few pastors and teachers.

About 444 B.C. the prophet Nehemiah paid a visit to Jerusalem, still in ruins from its destruction by Nebuchadnezzar more than a century before. The sight of the charred remains of the broken-down walls of the city saddened him. Like neo-Nehemiahs, today some have been out examining the theological walls of Zion and have concluded that they are likewise in disrepair and in need of restructuring. They feel that this doctrinal position is not as strong as some claim and that it requires outside reinforcement, specifically the writings of Ellen G. White, to bolster it. Such individuals feel that we should declare the teaching unsafe and vacate it.

In fact, some have argued that if we should find the investigative judgment faulty, creating a "breach in the bulwarks of belief," the whole citadel of Seventh-day Adventism is indefensible. Individuals have stated that if the teaching is erroneous, the Seventh-day

Adventist Church has no real purpose for existence and should quietly fold its clerical tent, since other groups practice, to one extent or another, its other doctrines, including Sabbathkeeping, healthful living, and a belief in an unconscious sleep at death. "If the foundations are destroyed, what can the righteous do?" (Ps. 11:3).

The challenges to the teachings of the pre-Advent judgment vary, but essentially they raise the objection that the doctrine does not rest on Scripture but must rely on the writings of Ellen White or church tradition for support. The Daniel 8:14 and investigative judgment criticisms involve the understanding of the number 2300; the application of the day-for-a-year principle; the teaching of a two-compartment heavenly sanctuary; the conflict between believing Christ waited until 1844 to enter the Most Holy Place though the Bible pictures Him in the Father's presence soon after His ascension; the translation and interpretation of the word "cleansed"; and the whole concept of a pre-Advent judgment in terms of God's omniscience. Our study won't consider all these concerns but will focus mainly on a comparison of biblical passages dealing with the judgment, a study of the word "cleansed" as used in Daniel 8:14, and an examination of various narratives that reveal God's pattern of investigating before He takes action.

We'll begin by observing the need for an investigative judgment and examining a model of heaven's judgment. Then our study will explore this subject from three different perspectives: *prophetic,* *linguistic,* and finally *narrative* points of view. In other words, we'll look at the prophecies of Daniel 8 and other Bible passages that bear on the issue, then take a closer view of the word "cleansed," and follow with a variety of stories in the Bible that demonstrate the character of God in action in real-life situations. Before we conclude, we'll take a very brief look at the issue of Christ being in His Father's presence after ascending and how that correlates with our topic. The question, then, is this: Does the Bible, without any outside support, teach a pre-Advent judgment? Is the historical understanding of the Adventist Church with regard to Daniel 8:14 sound? Is the Adventist Church on solid hermeneutical ground with respect to this doctrine?

Chapter One

The Necessity for a
Pre-Advent Judicial Review

Someone might be asking, especially if this topic is unfamiliar, What is the purpose of a judgment before Jesus comes back to earth? Why would a process of review be required? And so perhaps it would be helpful to lay a brief groundwork for the need of a pre-Advent investigative judgment. Let's take a look at some of the basic Bible teachings regarding our condition and God's process of salvation, because without an understanding of how He deals with sin and sinners, we will not grasp the relevance of the entire topic. Scripture reveals to us that:

1. All have sinned (Rom. 3:23).
2. Christ died for all (John 3:16; 1 John 2:2).
3. Anyone who accepts Christ's offer of salvation enjoys immediate forgiveness of sin, reconciliation with God, and "eternal life" (1 John 1:9; 5:11-13; 2 Cor. 5:18, 19) as Christ's righteousness covers the sins of the repentant believer.
4. This saved condition may be lost through apostasy if the believer falls away from grace (Heb. 10:38, 39).
5. A determination, therefore, must be made as to who, having confessed the name of Jesus, have retained their status of salvation (Rev. 22:11).

Because they relate directly to our study, let us consider the last three statements more particularly. In this computer age we can handle banking transactions, including transfers from one account to another, online. When I complete a transfer to my checking account, it gets posted immediately, and the verification indicates not only the date but even the exact time of day down to the minute, thus giving instantaneous credit. In the same way, the Bible teaches that a sinner who believes in Jesus is instantly credited with His righteousness (how interesting that the English word "credit" derives from the root "to believe"!) faster than when I hit Save on my PC. Heaven's accounting system instantly notes the transaction. Observe the present tense of the verbs in the following promises:

"Nevertheless do not rejoice in this, that the spirits are subject to you, but rather rejoice because your names are written in heaven" (Luke 10:20).

"And this is the testimony: that God has given us eternal life, and this life is in His Son. He who has the Son has life; he who does not have the Son of God does not have life. These things I have written to you who believe in the name of the Son of God, that you may know that you have eternal life" (1 John 5:11-13).

At this moment of time the child of God is in a saved position. Christ covers his or her sinful past. He's "whited-out" the sins of yesterday. But does this condition necessarily continue, or is there the possibility that a person may remove himself or herself from that saved condition? The Bible makes it clear that we can fall away from grace, can choose to remove ourselves from our saved condition. Since love is acceptable to Him only when given freely, God did not make us robots at birth, nor does He transform us into robots at rebirth. The power of choice remains with the individual both before and after coming to Him, with the attendant possibility that the person may decide to discontinue their walk in salvation. In accordance with this, the Word contains many admonitions to remain in Christ and not fall away:

"For we have become partakers of Christ if we hold the beginning of our confidence steadfast to the end" (Heb. 3:14).

"Let us therefore be diligent to enter that rest, lest anyone fall according to the same example of disobedience" (Heb. 4:11).

"'Now the just shall live by faith; but if anyone draws back, My soul has no pleasure in him.' But we are not of those who draw back to perdition, but of those who believe to the saving of the soul" (Heb. 10:38, 39).

"For if, after they have escaped the pollutions of the world through the knowledge of the Lord and Savior Jesus Christ, they are again entangled in them and overcome, the latter end is worse for them than the beginning. For it would have been better for them not to have known the way of righteousness, than having known it, to turn from the holy commandment delivered to them" (2 Peter 2:20, 21).

"Behold, I am coming quickly! Hold fast what you have, that no one may take your crown" (Rev. 3:11).

"When the righteous turns from his righteousness and commits iniquity, he shall die because of it" (Eze. 33:18).

So we see that Scripture describes salvation as a present reality for the believer, which may be forfeited. And what about having your name "written in heaven"? That sounds rather permanent, doesn't it? No, the Bible explains that it is possible to have your name removed from the book of life:

"If anyone takes away from the words of the book of this prophecy, God shall take away his part from the Book of Life, from the holy city, and from the things which are written in this book" (Rev. 22:19).

"And the Lord said to Moses, 'Whoever has sinned against Me, I will blot him out of My book'" (Ex. 32:33).

"Let them [persecutors] be blotted out of the book of the living, and not be written with the righteous" (Ps. 69:28).

Why would God caution us about having our name removed from the book of life if that was not a possibility? After all, a warning that foretells a consequence not based in fact damages the credibility of the individual giving the warning. When you were young and made those contorted facial expressions, maybe someone cautioned, "You'd better not do that, because your face may freeze that way." Then later you learned that there really is no basis in fact for such a thing, and so you doubted the word of the one who told you that. But God doesn't give groundless warnings. If He has told us that it is possible to have our name removed from the book of life, we conclude that it is so and that His warning is based in reality.

The example of King Saul illustrates how one might experience conversion and yet later fall away. The Bible states that the Spirit of the Lord came upon him and that he was "turned into another man" (1 Sam. 10:6), but later he fell to such a low state that the Lord wouldn't even speak to him (1 Sam. 28:6). Eventually Saul committed suicide. (Question: Was Judas among the group that day when the 70 returned and Jesus said, "Your names are written in heaven"?)

Why is it important to take time and effort to review this? Because we need to be clear that God's system of salvation places the believer into an immediate state of grace, with full pardon and entitlement to eternal life, including one's name being written in the book of life. At the same time, because God treasures freedom of choice so highly, believers retain their free will, and though it would break God's heart, it is possible for them to turn their backs on God and forfeit their right to salvation, with the subsequent removal of their inclusion in the book of life. Salvation has an Undo option that even a saved person can activate.

Jesus told a story one time involving a man who owed an enormous debt, so large it would have been impossible for him to ever pay it back. Because of this, as was the way of doing things back then, he, his wife and children, and all that he possessed were to be sold to satisfy the debt. So the man pleaded with the master. "Then the master of that servant was moved with compassion, released him, and forgave him the debt" (Matt. 18:27).

Subsequently this man, whom Jesus described as being "forgiven," found someone who owed him a small amount of money and began to demand payment. When the master found out about all this, he called him and said, "I forgave you all that debt. . . . Should you not also have had compassion on your fellow servant?" The master had him taken into custody and his whole debt reinstated (verses 32, 33). This man had been forgiven and his debt released, but his heartless misbehavior soon canceled his master's forgiveness. So it is true also that persons who confess Christ and have their sins covered by His righteousness, but later turn their backs on God and relinquish that covering, will then find the record of the past exposed and not forgiven.

During Old Testament times those who killed someone could escape the "avenger of blood" (a relative of the deceased, seeking justice) by fleeing to one of the six designated cities of refuge, there to await trial to determine if the homicide was intentional or not. Even after the hearing declared the person's innocence, it was necessary for the killer to *remain within* the city of refuge. "But if the manslayer at any time goes outside the limits of the city of refuge where he fled, and the avenger of blood finds him outside the limits of his city of refuge, and the avenger of blood kills the manslayer, he shall not be guilty of blood, because he should have remained in his city of refuge until the death of the high priest" (Num. 35:26-28).

Is this not a lesson of salvation, a warning that we need to remain "in Christ" and not wander away from the safety of His protection? We might then consider the believer's position as one of conditional salvation, just as the safety of the one who fled to the city of refuge was conditioned on his remaining within its walls until the death of the high priest guaranteed the person's safety (verse 28).

A look at some of the words the Bible uses to describe God's forgiveness might help us develop a model of how He deals with sin and sinners. One word is *kasah,* which has the basic meaning "to cover." "Blessed is he whose transgression is forgiven, whose sin is *covered"* (Ps. 32:1).

Another word is *kaphar.* It appears about 100 times and has a similar meaning of "covering" or "hiding" (see *The New Brown, Driver, Briggs, Gesenius Hebrew and English Lexicon* [BDBG], p. 497). Seventy times the KJV translates it as "atonement." "For the life of the flesh is in the blood, and I have given it to you upon the altar to make *atonement* for your souls; for it is the blood that makes *atonement* for the soul" (Lev. 17:11).

Job trusted that God would "plaster over" (the literal meaning of the Hebrew *taphal* translated "sewest up" in the KJV) his sin (Job 14:17). On the other hand, the Hebrew verb *machah* ("blot out," "wipe away," "efface," as in Exodus 32:33 and Psalm 69:28

above) many times seems to indicate a more permanent action.

The area where we live has many eucalyptus trees. I imagine that somehow long ago people noticed that these trees provide nice shade, because the word "eucalyptus" means literally "good covering." Christ is willing to provide a "good covering" for His sinful children with His robe of righteousness. How does the word "cover," in relation to the forgiveness of sins, shed light on "conditional salvation" and the need for an investigative judgment?

At our home we enjoy making greeting cards on our computer. It fascinates me that I can place an object on the page (let's say a picture of a person, or for the purpose of illustration, suppose it's the record of a person's sins), then acquire another image (for example, a lamb) and drag that image right over on top of the other picture so that we cannot see the first image (the record of sin) at all. The record is "covered" by the image of the lamb, even though technically it's still there underneath. Later I decide I don't like the lamb there, so I delete it, and, yes, the other image is still there, now visible because I have removed the lamb. It illustrates God's system of salvation, with immediate "coverage" by the Lamb available, but yet freedom of choice on our part to remove the Lamb.

We can see a statement Jesus made to the Jewish nation in this light: "O Jerusalem, Jerusalem, the one who kills the prophets and stones those who are sent to her! How often I wanted to gather your children together, as a hen gathers her chicks under her wings, but you were not willing!" (Matt. 23:37). Because they refused His "coverage," they left themselves exposed to the destroyer and unprotected.

But will this situation always continue, or will there be a time when decisions become finalized? Will the peace and serenity of eternity forever be limited and handicapped by a state of uncertainty because no choice has been ultimately decided? The Bible teaches clearly that death settles our destiny, causing "a great gulf" to be "fixed" (Luke 16:26). The wise man Solomon said, "In the place where the tree falls, there it shall lie" (Eccl. 11:3). But what about those alive when Jesus returns?

In the city of refuge model there came a time (the death of the high priest) when the verdict of not guilty became permanent. As long as Noah's ark was under construction the opportunity to choose continued, but eventually all who would had entered and the door had shut. Surely the process of finalization will have been completed before the return of Christ, with its resurrection of the sleeping saints and the translation of the living elect. Certainly at that time the redeemed will be forever saved.

So it is sensible to assume that at some point before this there would have been an inquiry as to who, among those who had accepted Christ (whether they have fallen asleep or are still alive when He comes back), have retained their saved condition. It stands to reason that there would come a time when all who have "continued to choose" God will have their decision forever recognized. It seems to reasonable minds that a finding would be made to see who, among those who acquired the image of the Lamb, have chosen to keep it and who have removed it, with their sins now exposed. There needs to be a review of the records—an investigative judgment.

Should it surprise us, then, that God, who is not the author of confusion, whose entire universe is in perfect organization, and who does all things "decently and in order" (1 Cor. 14:40), has arranged for a means of ascertaining all finalized decisions, to take place toward the very end of time, just prior to His return? We echo the sentiments of Abraham, who exclaimed, "Shall not the Judge of all the earth do right?" (Gen. 18:25). Should we not expect that with regard to such a significant undertaking—a concluding determination as to who will be saved—God would lay careful plans for such a vital accounting? In contrast to the farce of a trial that condemned the Son of God and was flawed by numerous illegalities, wouldn't we expect that God would conduct His legal work in an upright and aboveboard fashion?

No doubt you might be saying right now to yourself: "But God doesn't need to inquire—He already knows everything." And you're right! But as we shall see, it isn't for God's direct benefit that He does this. Besides, the Bible makes it clear that this process is something that God has definitely planned and predicted to take place.

Evidently before Jesus returns, such an evaluation will have taken place, because Scripture states that He will declare: "He who is unjust, let him be unjust still; he who is filthy, let him be filthy still; he who is righteous, let him be righteous still; he who is holy, let him be holy still. And behold, I am coming quickly, and My reward is with Me, to give to every one according to his work" (Rev. 22:11, 12).

Notice that the form of the verb in verse 11 is what scholars call *jussive imperative.* This text is not describing God as commanding the destiny of the individual. The judgment isn't God choosing who will be saved or lost, but rather His recognizing those who have themselves chosen to be saved or lost. Appropriately, then, the form of the verb is what is called *third person imperative,* translated by the phrase "let him," indicating God's recognition that each has made a final, irreversible decision for or against Him. God therefore states, "Let him *remain* saved or unsaved."

So we see that God has made provision for all sinners. Those who accept salvation receive eternal life immediately but can later renounce their decision, except that, for the purpose of bringing all things to closure, there will come a time when the Lord will announce all decisions as final. Let us study what the Scriptures reveal about this important event.

Chapter Two

A Model
of Heaven's Judgment

Keep in mind, as we study this topic, that Seventh-day Adventists believe that the heavenly judgment divides into at least three phases. Prior to Christ's second coming, the first, or *investigative phase,* of the judgment will convene in heaven. It will review the records and evidence, then reach a conclusion and pronounce a verdict.

As we study the scriptural portrayal of the judgment, we discover that even though the "Ancient of Days" presides (Dan. 7:9), Jesus is the judge. "For the Father judges no one, but has committed all judgment to the Son" (John 5:22). It is appropriate and comforting to know that the Judge has experienced life on this earth and is well acquainted with temptation and trial. Second, we find that Jesus is not only our judge but also our attorney. "My little children, these things I write to you, so that you may not sin. And if anyone sins, we have an Advocate with the Father, Jesus Christ the righteous" (1 John 2:1).

The Greek word translated "advocate" is *paraclete,* which means literally "one called to the side of." It is also the literal meaning of the word "advocate" (from the Latin *ad,* meaning "to," and *voc,* meaning "call"). This is the same word Scripture uses to describe the Holy Spirit as "Comforter." Those acquainted with today's court scene, so often polluted by chicanery and trickery, will find it reassuring to know that our attorney is Jesus Christ, one absolutely worthy of our trust and one who presents our case in the confidence of unfailing success.

Third, we see that Jesus is the "Faithful and True Witness"

(Rev. 3:14). In contrast to the many perversions of justice brought about in earthly courtrooms by the deceitful testimony of those sworn to tell "the truth, the whole truth, and nothing but the truth," how refreshing to rely on the unerring testimony of the one who *is* the truth. And to what does Jesus witness in this tribunal? It is that we have believed on and confessed His name, that we have accepted His offer of salvation, and that our lives bear testimony to being His sons and daughters: "Therefore whoever confesses Me before men, him I will also confess before My Father who is in heaven" (Matt. 10:32).

Last, Jesus is also, by substitution, the accused, having voluntarily taken our place. Through the miracle of divine grace Christ stands in our stead. "For He made Him who knew no sin to be sin for us, that we might become the righteousness of God in Him" (2 Cor. 5:21).

"Surely He has borne our griefs and carried our sorrows; yet we esteemed Him stricken, smitten by God, and afflicted. But He was wounded for our transgressions, He was bruised for our iniquities" (Isa. 53: 4, 5).

According to this model, with Jesus as the judge, the attorney, the witness, and the accused, we treasure the words of the Savior, who said: "Most assuredly, I say to you, he who hears My word and believes in Him who sent Me has everlasting life, and *shall not come into judgment,* but has passed from death into life" (John 5:24). No wonder John exclaimed that when our faith and love in Him are made perfect, we have no fear of the judgment (1 John 4:17, 18)!

Jesus stands in for the repentant sinner, and His merits replace the record of transgression, which results in heaven pronouncing a "not guilty" verdict in favor of the believer, a process that concludes before Jesus returns. Yes, the case of every person will be addressed, but even in our human court systems the parties involved are not physically present at all times. Sometimes the attorney represents someone who is absent. It is possible to understand Paul's statement that we will "all stand before the judgment seat of Christ" (Rom. 14:10) in this light. Though we may not be there physically when this aspect of the judgment occurs, we are there in the sense that our cases are being heard.

Subsequent to the termination of this phase of the judgment, Christ returns in glory to earth. Since the Bible describes Him as coming with His reward (see Isa. 40:10) we might think of this part of the judgment that occurs at the Second Advent as the beginning of the executive phase of the judgment—the implementing of the decisions resulting from the investigation. The word "executive" in this context means "putting into action." The righteous receive the reward of immortality at this time, as the dead in Christ are resurrected incorruptible and the living righteous are changed to incorruptible, and together as one group they meet their Lord in the air (1 Thess. 4:16, 17; 1 Cor. 15:51-55).

When Jesus comes back, then, one part of the judgment's verdict toward the righteous will have been enacted. The quality of the immortality they receive at this time will not be any different from the immortality they enjoy following the millennium. However, the full effect of God's plan toward the saved, including the re-creation of the earth as their final home, will take place after the period of the thousand years.

By a similar line of reasoning, God will have partially implemented the result of the judgment toward the wicked at Christ's return, since at that time the wicked dead are not resurrected, nor are the wicked who are alive translated to glory. It therefore will be clear to all when Jesus returns that those not taken to heaven will be forever lost. However, the full effect of the judgment against the wicked will likewise await the conclusion of the thousand years, when the second death will forever banish them from God's presence.

Another part of the judgment we might call the *millennial phase.* Seventh-day Adventists believe that following Christ's coming, during the period of 1,000 years, the righteous will have the opportunity to review for themselves the books of record in heaven to satisfy themselves as to the just administration of every case (Rev 20:4, 5).

What about the judgment scene portraying the "great white throne"? When does it take place, and whose cases are being tried at this time? The context of this passage, recorded in Revelation

20:11-15, best fits into the period following the period of 1,000 years but before God recreates our earth and makes everything new. Notice that just before this scene unfolds, verse 7 says, "Now when the thousand years have expired . . ." According to this timetable Christ has taken the saved to heaven a millennium before, and they have been reigning with Him (verse 6). The saints were either alive when Jesus returned to this earth and were "translated" to heaven without experiencing death, as was Enoch (Heb. 11:5), or they were raised from death in what the Bible calls the "first resurrection," the one in which the participants are "blessed and holy," and that the "second death has no power" (Rev. 20:5, 6) over.

The individuals being judged in Revelation 20:11-15 must therefore be the lost, described earlier in verse 5 as being "the rest of the dead." They either were in their graves at the time Jesus returned and did not hear His call to come to life, or were alive at the time of the Advent but were slain by "the brightness of His coming" (2 Thess. 2:8). The statement "but [in contrast to the righteous, who live and reign with Christ for 1,000 years] the rest of the dead did not live again until the thousand years were finished" (Rev. 20:5) intimates their return to life. (The NIV reads: "The rest of the dead did not *come to life* until the thousand years were ended.") At that time the second resurrection (a term suggested by the resurrection of the saints being called the "first resurrection" in Revelation 20:5), the "resurrection of condemnation" (John 5:29) that Jesus spoke about, now takes place, and the wicked face the implementation of their final judgment.

In a sense their cases have already been decided by process of elimination, because they are not among the saved. In the investigative phase of the judgment, which has taken place before Christ's return, either their names have been entered into the Lamb's book of life but later "blotted out" as ineligible because of their apostasy, or their names have never been written there at all. Since all humans are sinners and stand under the condemnation of sin, with its punishment of death, the only way to escape this penalty is to have Jesus' righteous record put in place of our sinful one. It is true that Jesus "saved" everyone at the cross, but His atonement is effectual only for those who believe in Him and accept His generous provision.

"He who believes in Him is not condemned; but he who does not believe is condemned already, because he has not believed in the name of the only begotten Son of God" (John 3:18).

In May 2000 Irish golfer Padraig Harrington was practicing a few putts before beginning the fourth and final round of the Benson and Hedges International Open in Sutton Coldfield, England. He enjoyed a five-stroke lead over his nearest rivals, Jose Maria Olazabal and Phillip Price, and appeared poised to capture the trophy and the first place prize of $252,000. When he looked up and saw senior referee Andy McFee approaching him, he sensed something was wrong.

It seems that Harrington had neglected to sign his scorecard from the first round of the tournament the previous Thursday, meaning that officially he hadn't played the round at all and therefore was immediately disqualified. By the same token, his course record-breaking 64 on Saturday "didn't happen."

Referee McFee didn't argue with Harrington, or even pull out a rulebook. He simply showed Harrington his Thursday's scorecard and sadly asked a question that will likely haunt Harrington for a long time: "Can you find your name there?"

Poor Harrington! He knew the rule and had no basis whatsoever to challenge it. Without his signature on the card it was impossible for him to be eligible to win the prize. He packed his putter and the rest of his clubs and left, searching for words to explain to his family and friends how the oversight could have happened.

In the same way, many will find themselves not able to qualify for eternal life, the biggest prize of all. Pointing to the book of life, God will sadly ask, "Can you find your name there?" Without their names ever having been written in the book of life they have no chance to qualify for salvation. "He who does not believe is condemned already."

Or we might think of it this way: a class-action lawsuit invites those concerned about a certain situation to submit their claims and participate in an award to be divided among the plaintiffs. If, having received the invitation but neglecting to answer, I later attempt to advance a claim after the case is adjudicated, disappointment will be the result. The judge will not even consider my participation in the award, because I had not submitted my request in a timely manner. Thus, according to the words of Jesus, some will be lost since they had not requested to be included in Jesus' favorable judgment through believing in the Son of God.

We might think of the "great white throne" judgment scene as depicting a final capstone on God's judicial system. The saved have already been enjoying immortality, and the process of elimination has already dealt with the lost. And now, for the first and only time, all of Adam's family—both the righteous and the resurrected wicked—are alive together. It will be at this time, in recognition of God's immutable justice and generous provision for salvation, that "every knee [shall] bow" (Phil. 2:10).

If this judgment primarily deals with the lost, then why do we find the book of life mentioned in this context? It verifies that the names of the lost are not written in it, and thus their fate—the second death—is justified.

With these different aspects of heaven's judgment in mind, we will focus our attention on the investigative phase, that part of the judgment that involves the opening of the record books before Jesus comes back to earth.

Chapter Three

The Investigative Judgment From a Prophetic Point of View

The Comparative Prophecies of Daniel 7 and 8

What we will see in this part of our study is that Daniel 7 portrays a "judgment scene" that precedes Christ's advent, and that the "cleansing of the sanctuary" of Daniel 8:14 is another term to describe the same event.

To lay the groundwork for comparing one prophecy with another, let's look first at the principle of *repetitive prophecy,* a vital concept in our study. Repetition is an important tool that the Sacred Record frequently uses. We're all acquainted with the adage that says "We learn by repetition." Repetition is a pattern that appears frequently in the Bible. For example, the Bible itself begins with two parallel accounts of creation (see Gen. 1:1-2:3; 2:4-25), the second building upon and amplifying the first.

Think back for a minute to when Joseph as a youth received the two dreams recorded in Genesis 37. In one dream, as he and his brothers were out in the field tying off bundles of grain, the sheaves belonging to his brothers bowed down and gave honor to Joseph's sheaf. Then Joseph had a second dream, and he related that now the sun, moon, and 11 stars paid homage to him. Though the two dreams employed different symbols (sheaves and stars), the *message* of the two dreams was obviously the same. They both foretold the future homage that Joseph's family would give him when he became prime minister of Egypt.

It was not Joseph's only encounter with two dreams conveying the same message. Later, when he was in Egypt, you will remember that the king summoned him to interpret his two dreams. In one dream Pharaoh saw seven well-fed cows feeding in a meadow, followed by seven skinny cows. Although the latter ate up the seven fat cows, they still remained thin. Then Pharaoh had a second dream, involving seven plump ears of grain, followed by seven withered and emaciated ears. Joseph correctly noted that the dream of the grain and the dream of the cows, although using different objects and given separately, were essentially saying the same thing, prompting his analysis that "the dreams of Pharaoh are one" (Gen. 41:25). The two dreams shared a congruent message, one repeated for emphasis. These episodes serve as examples of the *principle of repetition in prophecy.*

On more than one occasion God has repeated an important message and used different sets of symbols, at times working from the simple to the complex. The four "outline" visions of Daniel follow that paradigm, as do the visions of Revelation. They are *repetitive,* not consecutive. *Each* of the visions of Daniel takes us from the "present" (Daniel's day) to the "end."

Inasmuch as these visions cover the same basic material, they lend themselves to *comparative analysis.* Let's suppose that someone handed you these two lists:

List 1: cap, shirt, slacks, socks, and sandals.

List 2: hat, chemise, skirt, nylons, and shoes.

It is reasonable to assume that you would compare the two lists and come to some conclusions. First you might deduce that the two lists not only both contain articles of clothing, but that they appear in a specific order—from head to foot. As you examine the lists, even though you might not know the meaning of the word "chemise," you might be willing to accept it as a synonym of "shirt" because of its sequence in the list. "Chemise" *stands in the place* of "shirt," and since there seems to be a definite arrangement of the items, you think to yourself, *I will presume that a chemise must be some kind of shirt or blouse, unless there is evidence to the contrary.*

This is an example of comparative analysis, a method of study we can apply to the visions given in Daniel, because as we line up the individual symbolic items in the visions, we see a similarity, a pattern, that helps us reach certain conclusions.

You'll remember that Daniel 2 contains a vision featuring a great statue composed of different types of metal. The head of gold sits atop a chest of silver, a midsection of bronze, legs of iron, and feet of iron mixed with clay. We do not have to guess the meaning of the dream since Daniel goes on to explain that the head of gold represents Babylon, followed by another kingdom depicted by the silver chest. Historians agree that the Babylonian kingdom ruled by Nebuchadnezzar fell to the kingdom of the Medes and Persians. The kingdom of the Greeks, represented by the belly and thighs of bronze, in turn conquered it, only to capitulate to the Romans, symbolized by the legs of iron. The smashing of the feet by the stone foretells the coming of Christ's kingdom. If we were to reduce the statue dream of Daniel 2 to a list, the prophetic items would be:

Daniel 2

Four world empires

The breakup of the fourth empire

The destruction of earthly kingdoms

God's kingdom established

As we examine the vision of Daniel 7 we can likewise abbreviate it to a list of component parts and then compare the two visions. Daniel 7:1-8 contains a panorama utilizing animals of prey as prophetic symbols. We find a winged lion, followed by a bear with three ribs in its mouth, then a winged leopard, and finally an indescribable beast with 10 horns, three of which get uprooted and replaced by a manlike horn that, though small at first, becomes great and persecutes the saints and blasphemes against God.

Then Daniel's view opens to a great "judgment scene" in heaven (Dan. 7:9, 10), with none less than the Ancient of Days presiding, attended by myriads of angelic hosts. Thrones are placed and books are opened. *Following this* (Dan. 7:11), the blasphemous horn power comes to a climactic and flaming end. The rest of the chapter is essentially further explanation of some of the details of the vision, focusing particularly on the activities of the horn power and the ultimate triumph of God and His kingdom. We should note that this explanatory section lays out a specific time sequence:

"The saints shall be given into his hand for a time and times and half a time. But the court shall be seated, and they shall take away his dominion, to consume and destroy it forever. Then the kingdom and dominion, and the greatness of the kingdoms under the whole heaven, shall be given to the people, the saints of the Most High" (verses 25-27).

Here we see the broad outline of Daniel 7 fleshed out a little more than the statue of chapter 2:

Daniel 2	Daniel 7
Four world empires	Four world empires
The breakup of the fourth	The breakup of the fourth
	Emergence of the horn power
	Heaven's court convenes
Destruction of earthly	The horn power destroyed
kingdoms	
God's kingdom established	God's kingdom established

With respect to the first four animals, Bible scholars for centuries have had little difficulty in identifying them as the monarchies of Babylon, Medo-Persia, Greece, and Rome. Concerning the horn power, which started out small but became big, Seventh-day Adventists stand in a long and illustrious line of expositors, including most of the Reformers, in recognizing the horn power as the medieval church, with its bombastic claims to equality with God, including the ability to forgive sins and change His law. It has a sad history of persecuting those whose consciences forbade them to accept the teachings and authority of the Roman Church.

As we compare the statue from the vision in the second chapter with the animals of prey in the seventh chapter, we see several points of comparison. The two lists seem to be similar. We see four great monarchies outlined, with Babylon being the head of gold in chapter 2 and the tawny winged lion in chapter 7. The silver chest in chapter 2 and the hunched-up bear of chapter 7, with three ribs in its mouth, represent Medo-Persia. Greece is the midsection of bronze in chapter 2 as well as the yellowish four-headed winged leopard of chapter 7. We recognize Rome as the legs of iron in chapter 2 and the iron-toothed monster of chapter 7. And the stone smashing the statue in chapter 2 parallels the kingdom's being given to the saints in chapter 7.

Both visions begin in Daniel's day and take us to the "end." But notice that chapter 7 adds several interesting details not introduced in chapter 2. From the seventh chapter we learn that the approaches of the first and third kingdoms occur with unusual speed, represented by the wings on the lion and leopard, a concept not conveyed in the statue portrayal.

In chapter 7 we learn that the second kingdom conquers three territories to gain its supremacy, represented by the three ribs, and that of this coalition government, one member achieves dominance, represented by the bear raised up on one side. After the fall of the fourth empire another power will ascend from its fragments, a religiopolitical system that will defy God, attempt to change His law, and persecute His children during an uninterrupted period of "a time and times and half a time." Chapter 7 also teaches us that after the conclusion of the persecutions God will convene His divine tribunal, that thrones will be established, and that heaven's record books will be opened prior to the triumphant deliverance of the saints and the final and ultimate destruction of the horn power and its followers.

Turning to Daniel 8, we find still another vision, this time utilizing animals of sacrifice in contrast to the unclean animals of prey in chapter 7. It depicts a ram sporting two horns, one higher than the other, and the higher one appearing last. The ram pushed *westward, northward,* and *southward,* and seemed invincible. Then "suddenly" a goat appeared from the *west* and seemed not to touch the ground in its swift approach. This goat had a remarkable horn that, following the trampling of the ram, became four horns that spread toward the four winds of heaven, or directions of the compass. From one of these *directions* (the pronoun "them" in Hebrew agrees more with the antecedent "wind" than "horn") there came another outstanding horn, whose domain grew toward the *south,* toward the *east,* and toward the *"Glorious Land."* Then this horn behaved in a highly destructive manner. It trampled some of the "stars," exalted itself against the Prince of the host, removed the daily sacrifices, erased the place of His sanctuary, and cast truth to the ground. In the process it prospered wonderfully.

As we study the vision in the eighth chapter the obvious conclusion is that the basic message is the same as in the other presentations: kingdoms will come and kingdoms will go; earthly powers will assert themselves against God, His system, and His people; but the ultimate victory of God and His saints is assured. The destructive horn power will be "broken without human means" (Dan. 8:25).

This chapter specifically identifies the ram and the goat: they represent the kingdoms of Medo-Persia and Greece, respectively. It also passes some new information along, informing us that with respect to the coalition government of the Medes and Persians, the dominant one comes to authority last, represented by the higher horn on the ram. Daniel 8 introduces us to the mighty ruler of Greece, without question foretelling the success of Alexander the Great, the "notable horn" that stands out.

Having already digested the visions of the second and seventh chapters, we are now prepared to employ some comparative analysis techniques as we attempt to achieve further understanding. A question comes to mind: Why do we find only two animals in this vision, while the statue of Daniel 2 depicted four kingdoms and Daniel 7 presented four animals plus a dominant horn power? Since the book of Daniel clearly tells us that the ram of chapter 8 represents the rulers of Media and Persia (Dan. 8:20), we conclude that Babylon has, for all intents and purposes—at least in God's way of looking at it—passed from the scene of action. Because of its continued rebellion against heaven it will soon fill its cup of iniquity and receive divine judgment. Even though the prophet receives his vision in the third year of the reign of Belshazzar, which chronologists have suggested would be 550/549 B.C., or about 10 years before Babylon's fall, it had already sealed its doom and was no longer the concern of divine prophecy, just as you no longer water November's tomato plant. Indeed, Daniel in his vision saw himself not in Babylon, where no doubt he was physically, but in

Persia as the scene unfolded by the banks of the Ulai River in Shushan. So that accounts for one of the "missing" kingdoms, but what about the other?

As we become acquainted with this prophecy we sense a strong emphasis placed on *direction,* or *location,* in the language used. We observe specific (and very accurate!) geographical references made to the activities of the ram and of the goat. Certainly the armies of Alexander came from the *west* as they attacked Persia, just as in the vision the goat approached from the west.

Then we notice that out of one of the "winds," or directions of the compass (the "four winds of heaven" is a frequent idiom used to denote the four directions of the compass), rises a horn power whose activities, attitudes, and final destruction echo the horn power of the seventh chapter. Observe these points of comparison between the horn power of Daniel 7 and the horn power of Daniel 8:

1. Both achieved remarkable growth and influence. In chapter 7 it was "little" in its beginning (Dan. 7:8) but then became "greater than his fellows" (verse 20). Chapter 8 states that the horn power "grew exceedingly great" (Dan. 8:9).

2. The horn power fiercely persecuted God's people. In the vision of chapter 7 it "was making war against the saints, and prevailing against them" (Dan. 7:21), and the vision foretold that it would "persecute the saints of the Most High" and that they would be "given into his hand" (verse 25). Then in chapter 8 the horn "cast down some of the host and some of the stars to the ground, and trampled them" (Dan. 8:10) and the angel predicted that it would "destroy the mighty, and also the holy people" (verse 24).

3. The horn power directly confronted God. Thus in chapter 7 it spoke "pompous words against the Most High" (Dan. 7:25), while in chapter 8 it exalted itself as high as the "Prince of the host" (Dan. 8:11) and rose against the "Prince of princes" (verse 25).

Because direction or location seems to be a dominant theme in this presentation, we are prepared to test the theory that this horn represents Rome in *both its civil and papal manifestations.* In other words, since the caesars and popes both exercised authority from the same location, and because their behaviors were quite similar,

Scripture presents them through a combined symbol, that of the horn power. The legs of iron of the statue of Daniel 2 and the monstrous beast of chapter 7 *are* there in chapter 8, but within the broader symbol of the horn power.

History bears out in many ways that what *civil Rome did in a literal way, papal Rome repeated in a spiritual way.* Take note of the following five points of comparison:

1. Civil Rome stretched out its arm of world dominion in a remarkable way, as did papal Rome later, a fact depicted by the stupendous growth of the horn power.

2. Civil Rome persecuted many of the Christian leaders, as witnessed by the Colosseum and the catacombs, just as did papal Rome later, evidenced by the Inquisition and crusades against dissident groups.

3. Civil Rome exalted itself against the Prince of the host, inasmuch as it was under Roman authority that Christ was crucified. Papal Rome has proclaimed that as God's representative on earth it is equal with God and therefore has the authority to change His law.

"The Pope is of so great dignity and so exalted he is not a mere man, but as it were God, and the vicar of God. . . . The Pope can modify divine law, since his power is not of man but of God, and he acts as vicegerent of God upon earth . . ." (translated from the writings of the eighteenth-century Roman Catholic Lucius Ferraris, *Prompta Bibliotheca,* Vol. VI, pp. 25-29).

4. Because of Christ's death on the cross under the authority of civil Rome, the daily sacrifices in the Temple, with animals being put to death as a symbol of the one who was to come, reached their fulfillment and came ultimately to an end, a fact symbolized by the Temple curtain's ripping from top to bottom as the real Lamb of God gave His life. It is true that for a few decades the offering of sacrificial animals in the Temple continued, and even the apostle Paul participated in such services (Acts 21:20-26). Although they didn't come to their literal end until the destruction of Jerusalem in A.D. 70, it could be argued that as far as God was concerned, "type had met antitype" when Jesus died on the cross, and there-

fore the daily sacrifice had been removed and the "house" was desolate. Papal Rome has removed the "daily" by promoting a concept of salvation rooted in human merit in place of the divine provision represented by Jesus' blood.

5. Civil Rome destroyed the literal place of His sanctuary when it sacked Jerusalem in A.D. 70 under the generalship of Titus. Papal Rome "destroyed the sanctuary" by substituting for the divine method of dealing with sin (the express purpose for the sanctuary service) a human pronouncement ("I forgive you") in the priestly confessional (for the Catholic teaching on the priests' authority to forgive, see, for example, *The Faith Of Our Fathers,* by James Cardinal Gibbons [New York: National Headquarters of the Holy Name Society, 1929], pp. 339-369).

And what about the "heavenly judgment scene" that takes place before the end, so vividly portrayed in Daniel 7, with its thrones put in place and its books under review? Where does that appear in chapter 8? Let's remember that the animals of chapter 8 are of a different class than those of chapter 7. Chapter 7 employs unclean animals, specifically beasts of prey. The Scriptures never mention lions, bears, or leopards as being used for sacrifice in the Temple. But in chapter 8 we have a ram and a goat, both of which are clean animals, animals often employed in sacrifice and thus frequently seen in the sanctuary. This in itself might be a clue to understanding the message of the vision of chapter 8, for we can make a strong argument that this vision reflects "the backdrop of the sanctuary" for the following reasons:

1. The animals in this chapter are those often used in sacrifice: a ram and a goat.

2. The destructive activity of the horn power focuses its attack against the "daily" sacrifices, a major rite.

3. The vision describes the war waged by the horn against God and His people through the phrase "the place of His sanctuary was cast down" (Dan. 8:11).

4. Daniel's prayer of response, in chapter 9, requests that "for the Lord's sake cause Your face to shine on Your sanctuary, which is desolate" (Dan. 9:17).

As we line up the symbols of the visions given in chapters 7 and 8 we see that the "cleansing of the sanctuary" of Daniel 8:14 stands in *the position* of the "judgment scene" of chapter 7, in which Daniel sees the books being opened in heaven. Both the "heavenly assize" of chapter 7 and the "cleansing of the sanctuary" of chapter 8 get introduced *after* the presentation of the world kingdoms, including a highly aggressive horn power, but *before* God brings the earthly kingdoms to their end.

The "judgment scene" of chapter 7 and the "cleansing of the sanctuary" of chapter 8 together represent the critical element that turns the tide, bringing about the end of the domination of earthly systems and the introduction of God's kingdom. As such, the importance of this event would be impossible to overestimate. Chapter 7 depicts earthly powers as having their way until the judgment scene is unveiled and God pronounces in favor of the saints. Likewise, in chapter 8 the earthly powers have the upper hand until the sanctuary is cleansed and then the horn is broken without hand.

Those who study the trends of the financial world look for that key economic report, that statement by the Federal Reserve Board, that changes the direction of the market. Sportscasters are fond of analyzing games in which it seems that momentum favors one team, only to have the other squad make a valiant comeback. Then they attempt to isolate that one play, that one moment, that was the pivot point that made the momentum shift and spelled the difference between victory or defeat for the resurging team. In the contest between good and evil, unfolded so graphically in the visions of Daniel, it is the "judgment scene" in chapter 7, the "cleansing of the sanctuary" in chapter 8, that comprises that critical moment that paves the way for the tables to turn in favor of the saints.

Daniel 7	Daniel 8
Four world empires	Two world empires
The breakup of the fourth	

Emergence of the horn power	Emergence of the horn power (civil and papal Rome)
Heaven's court convenes	Sanctuary is cleansed
Horn power is destroyed	Horn power is destroyed
God's kingdom established	

Because the "cleansing of the sanctuary" of chapter 8 *occupies the same place* in the order of the lists as does the "heavenly tribunal" of chapter 7 (that is, after the introduction of worldly kingdoms and before the final end, when the horn gets "broken without hand" [Dan. 8:25, KJV], an obvious echo of the stone "cut out without hands" that smashes the feet of the image of chapter 2), we are prepared to view it as another way of expressing the judgment review.

Since the backdrop or context of this chapter is the sanctuary, should we be surprised that the "judgment scene" portrayed in chapter 7 would in chapter 8 be expressed in a sanctuary context? That leads us to ask the question Was there a specific part of the sanctuary service that Scripture understood as having special application to judicial proceedings? The answer to this question is yes. It is known that the Jews looked upon Yom Kippur, the Day of Atonement, as the "day of judgment."

As I researched the Day of Atonement in Jewish literature, I was struck by how often a picture of a set of balance scales, a universal symbol of judgment, accompanied articles on the subject. Here are a few of the quotations I found with respect to the meaning of Yom Kippur as understood by Jews today:

"Yom Kippur, the Day of Atonement, is the most sacred of the Jewish holidays, the 'Sabbath of Sabbaths.'

"By Yom Kippur the 40 days of repentance, that begin with the first of Elul, have passed. On Rosh Hashanah G-d has judged most of mankind and has recorded his judgement in the Book of Life. But he has given a 10 day reprieve.

"On Yom Kippur the Book of Life is closed and sealed. Those that have repented for their sins are granted a good and happy New Year" (www.holidays.net/highholydays/yom.htm).

"Yom Kippur ('Day of Atonement') is the tenth day of the month of Tishrei. It is the holiest day of the Jewish year. On this day, G-d seals our fate for the coming year, therefore, the entire day is spent fasting and praying to G-d for forgiveness and a good year" (www.torah.org).

"Yom Kippur is considered the holiest of the Jewish holy days. . . . This is considered to be the time when the final verdict is made for each human life for the coming year" (www.amfi.org).

"In *Days of Awe* I mentioned the 'books' in which G-d inscribes all of our names. On Yom Kippur, the judgment entered in these books is sealed. This day is, essentially, your last appeal, your last chance to change the judgment, to demonstrate your repentance and make amends" (www.us-Israel.org/jsource/Judaism/holi-day4.html).

"The services [of Yom Kippur] close with the sounding of the shofar (ram's horn trumpet) symbolizing the closing of the heavenly gates. During the High Holy Days, God is said to bring His heavenly court into session to judge the deeds of mankind. Court opens with Rosh Hashana and closes with the final shofar blast of Yom Kippur. One hopes and prays one is *sealed* in the Book of Life at the close of Yom Kippur" (www.chaim.org/churches/yom.pdf).

"The final Yom Kippur service is called Ni' ilah (shutting) because of the prayer imagery, which refers to the 'shutting of the gates.' Jewish tradition regards Yom Kippur as the day on which God decides the fate of each human being. As the holiday comes to an end, the liturgy vividly depicts gates beginning to close.

"During the Ni' ilah service, people pray with special intensity, hoping to be admitted to God's loving presence before the gates leading to Him are closed" (www.shul.org).

"Jewish tradition looks to Yom Kippur as a day of judgment" (www.nd.edu).

A general agreement exists that the Jews understood Yom Kippur as representing a day of judgment in God's administration. It is entirely within reason, therefore, since chapter 8 of Daniel has a sanctuary context, and since the event described in verse 14 stands in the place of the "judicial scene" of chapter 7 in which

God opens the record books for review, that we remain open to the possibility that the "cleansing of the sanctuary" pertains to that part of the sanctuary service that functioned as a time of judgment, namely the Day of Atonement service. Thus, studying the parallel prophecies of Daniel 7 and 8 leads us to anticipate that a judgment of review will convene prior to Christ's return.

A Pre-Advent Judgment in Prophecy

What do other scriptures tell us of a judgment that will take place before Jesus comes back? Most Bible writers placed it in the future. Paul, witnessing to the Areopagites on Mars' Hill in Athens, said to them: "He has appointed a day on which He *will* judge the world in righteousness by the Man whom He has ordained" (Acts 17:31).

Appealing to Felix, the apostle "reasoned about righteousness, self-control, and the judgment *to come*" (Acts 24:25).

King Solomon, the wisest man of all, said: "For God *will bring* every work into judgment, including every secret thing, whether good or evil" (Eccl. 12:14).

All of these texts, and others, place the judgment in the future. And yet Revelation 14:6, 7 clearly pictures a time when the judgment (or at least one phase of it) is conducted and finalized prior to the return of Jesus: "Then I saw another angel flying in the midst of heaven, having the everlasting gospel to preach to those who dwell on the earth—to every nation, tribe, tongue, and people—saying with a loud voice, 'Fear God and give glory to Him, for the hour of His judgment *has come.'*"

The prophecy of Revelation 14 doesn't depict the return of Christ until verse 14, which pictures the Lord coming back with His sickle to reap the earth's harvest. In other words, preparatory to Christ's advent an announcement will circle the globe that the heavenly tribunal has convened. That part of the judgment that the prophet Daniel saw in vision (recorded in Daniel 7:9, 10, with its books of judgment opened) will commence and conclude before Jesus returns. If language means anything, Revelation 14 clearly highlights a part of the judgment as taking place before the Second Advent.

At that time God investigates human affairs for the purposes of human salvation or destruction. It is not that He doesn't already have the capacity to know the outcome of every human case. But to assure those who are not omniscient as He is, to give evidence even beyond what is necessary that He is thorough and fair and that He bases His decisions on trustworthy knowledge, *He investigates before He takes action.* He greatly desires His creatures to be at ease with regard to the verdicts rendered, and so He condescends to go the second mile for the purpose of inspiring confidence in His leadership.

This concept agrees with what John reported Jesus as saying in the very last chapter of the Bible, that when He comes back, all decisions have been finalized, and that He brings His reward with Him (Rev. 22:12). The fact that He already has the appropriate reward with Him makes the best sense if understood in the light of an investigative judgment having concluded prior to the time when Jesus returns to earth.

Another text that best fits within this perspective is Daniel 12:1: "And at that time your people shall be delivered, every one who is found written in the book."

Consider for a moment the phrase "found written in the book." What book does the passage have in mind? It is obviously the book of life, containing the names of those whom God will save. Why did the vision promise Daniel deliverance for his people, those "written in the book," if there was to be no *looking into* the book to see whose names were there? Doesn't the word "found" indicate a search or examination? You don't usually describe something as being found unless someone conducted a search for it. Within the shell of the word "found" lies the seed of the word "search."

On one occasion, just after we had moved into a new house, I wasn't able to locate my hammer. It was special to me because it had belonged to my dad. I searched high and low but couldn't put my hands on it. Years later, when we were moving from that house, I discovered it resting on a window sill concealed by curtains in an out-of-the-way hall window. Evidently I had used it to tack up the curtain rod brackets and had left it there. How happy

I was to finally find it! Thus, inherent in the word "found" in Daniel 12:1 is the concept of "look" or "inquest" that is fulfilled by the investigative judgment.

For a moment, let's attempt to reconcile the concept of God's omniscience with this judgment that involves the opening of books. Without question, one of the prerogatives of divinity that Scripture applies to God is omniscience. God knows all. His knowledge and memory are unfailing. Nothing can be hidden from His view. He is perfect in wisdom: "I am God, and there no other; I am God, and there is none like Me, declaring the end from the beginning, and from ancient times things that are not yet done" (Isa. 46:9, 10).

"O Lord, You have searched me and known me. You know my sitting down and my rising up; You understand my thought afar off. You comprehend my path and my lying down, and are acquainted with all my ways. For there is not a word on my tongue, but behold, O Lord, You know it altogether" (Ps. 139:1-4).

"If I say, 'Surely the darkness shall fall on me,' even the night shall be light about me; indeed, the darkness shall not hide from You, but the night shines as the day; the darkness and the light are both alike to You" (Ps. 139:11, 12).

"The Lord looks from heaven; He sees all the sons of men. From the place of His dwelling He looks on all the inhabitants of the earth; He fashions their hearts individually; He considers all their works" (Ps. 33:13-15).

The Scriptures plainly teach that the Lord is all-knowing. We might ask then, Since God is omniscient and has a perfect memory, what *is* the function of the books opened in the judgment scene depicted in Daniel 7? Why have books or records at all? Notice this point very carefully: If I reject the Bible teaching of a judgment before the Second Advent, deciding that it is useless, given God's omniscience, I might as well reject the Bible's description of books of judgment for the same reason. We might as well retrieve Jehoiakim's penknife (see Jer. 36:1-3, 22, 23) and cut out of our Bibles references to the "book of life" and the "book of remembrance," as well as the books mentioned in Daniel 7 opened for judgment. On the other hand, if it is true that heavenly record books do exist, then why would it be difficult to grasp their being opened and examined?

If God knows everything, we might see no need for Him to keep records. And yet the Bible clearly speaks of them. Is it not for the sake of those whose minds and memories are not like God's? Again we say, God certainly has the ability to know who will be saved and lost, yet He lowers Himself to conduct His affairs in ways that create confidence in His leadership. He investigates before He takes action.

Prophetic Study Summary

On this part of our journey we have seen that the Bible describes one aspect of the judgment as taking place before Christ's return, when He opens the heavenly record books for review. This is entirely reasonable, because when He comes, it is "with His reward." We have observed that what happens at the conclusion of the 2300-day prophecy of Daniel 8 stands in the position of the "judicial review" described by Daniel 7, and that therefore we can regard the "cleansing of the sanctuary" as an alternate expression for this pre-Advent judgment.

As a result we conclude that it is reasonable to connect the "cleansing of the sanctuary" and the Day of Atonement service, given the sanctuary backdrop of Daniel 8, particularly since Jews have long understood the Day of Atonement as a time of judgment that seals every person's destiny. It is a concept that agrees with the Seventh-day Adventist position regarding the antitypical significance of the Day of Atonement.

Chapter Four

Learning About the Investigative Judgment From a Word Study of "Cleansed"

Words are the building blocks of language. In the book of Galatians Paul developed a whole theology on not just one word but whether that one word ("seed") was singular or plural (Gal. 3:16). Therefore, taking into account the importance of this topic, we would do well to carefully examine the key verb of our text. Let's put the spotlight on the key verb of Daniel 8:14, translated "cleansed" in the KJV.

As we read the passage in different English translations of the Bible, we encounter a variety of verbs used to close the verse. In the place of the sanctuary being "cleansed," the KJV and NKJV rendition, other versions read, for example:

"He said to me, 'It will take 2,300 evenings and mornings; then the sanctuary will be reconsecrated'" (NIV).

"And he said to him, 'For two thousand and three hundred evenings and mornings; then the sanctuary shall be restored to its rightful state'" (RSV).

"And he said to me, 'For 2,300 evenings and mornings; then the holy place will be properly restored'" (NASB, with the margin reading "vindicated" for "restored").

"He answered him, 'For two thousand three hundred evenings and mornings; then the sanctuary shall be purified'" (NAB).

Because the verb "cleansed" is absent from these reputable translations (although the NAB "purified" is close), one wonders if "cleansed" is an appropriate translation of the Hebrew verb. If it is, why would not the new translations follow the KJV? But if "cleansed" is a translation that begs for improvement, could it be that the Seventh-day Adventist view of this prophecy, which links it with the Day of Atonement service (based on its being "cleansed"), is also in need of improvement? Critics of the Adventist teaching of the investigative judgment say yes and argue that support for the translation "cleansed" is thin and that we have used it unfairly to connect Daniel 8:14 to the Day of Atonement service, which has the sanctuary "cleansed." Could it be that the concept of a pre-Advent judgment based on this view is erroneous?

Just what Hebrew word appears in this verse, what does it mean, and, perhaps more important, how does the rest of the Bible use it? Is "cleansed" a legitimate translation of the Hebrew? Does the Hebrew word employed in Daniel 8:14 have any association with the concept of judicial proceedings?

Dictionary Definition Of *Tsadaq* ("Cleansed")

With these thoughts in mind, let us turn our attention to the word in question. We'll start with the dictionary definition and then look to see how the Old Testament employs it elsewhere. The Hebrew word appearing in Daniel 8:14 and rendered "cleansed" in the KJV (and NKJV) is the verb *tsadaq,* which *The New Brown, Driver, Briggs and Gesenius Hebrew and English Lexicon* defines as:

"*Be just, righteous.* (Qal—simple active) 1. *have a just cause, be in the right;* 2. *be justified,* in one's plea, by witnesses, by acquittal, by condemnation of opponent; 3. *be just,* of God in His government, in charging with sin; 4. *be just, righteous,* in conduct and character

"(Niphal—passive) *to be put right,* in a right condition; *to be justified,* its cause vindicated

"(Piel—intensive) *to justify;* make appear righteous

"(Hiphael—causative) 1. *do justice,* in administering law; 2. *declare righteous, justify;* 3. *justify, vindicate the cause of, save;* 4. *make righteous, turn to righteousness*

"(Hithpael—reflexive) *justify ourselves,* clear ourselves from suspicion"

From the dictionary definition we can see that the broad concept of the Seventh-day Adventist position, though not spelled out in detail, is nevertheless implicit. The lexicographers have recognized that this word expresses legal function and conveys a court or legal connotation. It's a word you can very well use in describing what takes place in a judgment setting.

Contextual Study of *Tsadaq* ("Cleansed")

But perhaps even more instructive than dictionary definitions is what we find when we look at the ways that Bible writers use the word in actual contexts. We can let the Bible be its own dictionary by comparing scripture with scripture, allowing the book to teach us the meaning of the word in other texts. Studying the word within contexts has the advantage of allowing us to grasp the flavor, or larger connotation, of a particular word.

A Listing of the Old Testament Occurrences of *Tsadaq*

For the sake of completeness (and despite the risk of being tedious), here is an entire listing of the texts containing this verb. I invite the reader to study each incidence and form their own conclusions about the "flavor" of the word. After citing them, we will highlight a few. According to Robert Young's *Analytical Concordance to the Bible,* the verb appears 41 times, and the KJV translates it in the following ways:

1. From the qal, or simple active voice:
   "be just" (three times: Job 4:17; 9:2; 33:12, KJV)
   "be justified" (eight times: Job 11:2; 13:18; 25:4; Ps. 51:4; 143:2; Isa. 43:9, 26; 45:25)
   "be righteous" (10 times: Gen. 38:26; Job 9:15; 10:15; 15:14; 22:3; 34:5; 35:7; 40:8; Ps. 19:9; Ezek. 16:52, KJV)
   "justify self" (one time: Job 9:20, KJV)
2. From the niphal, or passive voice:
   "be cleansed" (one time: Dan. 8:14, KJV)
3. From the piel, or intensive voice:
   "justify" (five times: Job 32:2; 33:32; Jer. 3:11; Eze. 16:51, 52, KJV)
4. From the hiphal, or causative voice:
   "do justice" (two times: 2 Sam. 15:4; Ps. 82:2, 3, KJV)
   "justify" (nine times: Ex. 23:6, 7; Deut. 25:1; 1 Kings 8:32;

2 Chron. 6:23; Job 27:5; Prov. 17:15; Isa. 5:23; 50:8; 53:11, KJV)
  "turn to righteousness" (one time: Dan. 12:3, KJV)
  5. From the hithpael, or reflexive voice:
    "clear selves" (one time: Gen. 44:16, KJV)

To be fair, we notice initially that the KJV employs "cleansed" only once, that is, in Daniel 8:14, while "be justified," "be righteous" and "justify" appear the majority of the time.

From the way the Old Testament employs the word, what can we learn about it and the linguistic clothing it wears? What is the broader connotation it conveys? What kind of picture does the word paint? Does it support the kind of interpretation Seventh-day Adventists place upon it, that of portraying a judicial setting in which heaven conducts an investigation and reviews evidence for the purpose of exonerating the innocent and vindicating the righteous? What would be the effect of transferring the connotation of the verb as it appears elsewhere in Scripture to Daniel 8:14? Is the "cleansed" translation of the KJV a reasonable one, or should we disregard it altogether and instead look exclusively toward one of the words that modern translations use?

Comments on the Usages of *Tsadaq*

We'll divide our comments on the usages of tsadaq into two categories: those that show a kinship to the words "clean" or "cleansed," since that is the way the KJV translates *tsadaq* in Daniel 8:14 (a rendition some have objected to), and those in which the context clearly demonstrates a judicial or courtroom environment.

Tsadaq and "Clean"

As we review the usages of *tsadaq,* we find five occurrences involving a close association with the words "clean," "clear," or "pure" (Job 4:17; 15:14; 25:4; Ps. 19:9; 51:4). The adage that says "You can tell a lot about a person by the company they keep" applies to words as well. The two Hebrew words *tahor* and *zakah,* both meaning "clean" or "pure," appear in these five verses, yoked to *tsadaq.*

Each of the five verses consists of Hebrew poetry, a fact reflected in the way that most modern translations print them. They are examples of *synonymous parallelism.* Synonymous parallelism means that the words of the first line of a couplet essentially say the same thing as those of the second part of the couplet. It isn't necessary to view the words or lines as being absolutely identical or congruent, because different words, even synonyms, have their own nuances. But their meaning is similar and close enough that we call the pattern synonymous parallelism. Hebrew poetry involved rhyme of *thought,* not of *sound.*

Recognizing the literary pattern allows us to reach certain conclusions regarding the usages of words found in such examples of synonymous parallelism. Thus in Job 4:17 the theme of the first line of the couplet:

"Can a mortal be more righteous than God?"
is repeated in the second half of the couplet:
"Can a man be more pure than his Maker?"

We see in this poetic example of synonymous parallelism that "man" in the second half echoes "a mortal" in the first half, "pure" parallels "righteous," and "Maker" corresponds with "God." The writer of the poem skillfully employs different words with similar meanings to craft his thoughts into a verse that has a "rhyme" of concept.

What is germane to our study is to notice that in the five passages under study, the Hebrew word *tsadaq,* translated "cleansed" in the KJV of Daniel 8:14, appears in a position of synonymous parallelism with other Hebrew words that mean "clean," "clear," or "pure." In the Job 4:17 example, we find "righteous" *(tsadaq)* in the first half reflected by "pure" *(tahor)* in the second half.

Psalm 19:9 offers another example of this type of synonymous parallelism: "The fear of the Lord is clean *(tahor),* enduring forever; the judgments of the Lord are true and righteous *(tsadaq)* altogether."

Before leaving the word *tahor,* we should point out that Scripture employs it to describe the purpose of the Day of

Atonement service, and the related Hebrew verb *taher* appears twice in Leviticus 16 in the context of Yom Kippur:

"He shall sprinkle some of the blood on [the horns of the altar] with his finger seven times, cleanse *(taher)* it, and consecrate it from the uncleanness of the children of Israel" (Lev. 16:19).

"For on that day the priest shall make atonement for you, to cleanse *(taher)* you, that you may be clean *(tahor)* from all your sins before the Lord" (verse 30).

How interesting that this word, the meaning of which is close enough to be used in a position of synonymous parallelism with *tsadaq,* Scripture here employs to describe the goal of the Day of Atonement service! Because of the usage of "cleanse" in Leviticus 16, it is natural to look upon Yom Kippur as the day the sanctuary was "cleansed" by symbolically removing from it the "reminder of sins" (Heb. 10:3). And because the words used in Leviticus 16 occur in a synonymous way with the key verb of Daniel 8:14, we find that neither the translation "cleansed" nor the link between Daniel 8:14 and the Day of Atonement service stretches the inherent meaning.

On a deeper level we might also note that the purpose of the festival was not just to cleanse the sanctuary but, ultimately, to cleanse the people. "That *you* may be clean" was really what God intended to achieve. It is of little consequence to Him to purify the furniture and building unless that act included with it the sanctifying of the human heart. For Him, the internal has always taken precedence over the external. Likewise, the cleansing of the heavenly sanctuary implies much more than merely God's applying the divine eraser to the records of human sin. "That *you* may be clean" must also be the end product of the antitypical day of atonement.

The other three texts under review use a different Hebrew word. Job 15:14 declares:

"What is man, that he could be pure *(zakah)?*

And he who is born of a woman, that he could be righteous *(tsadaq)?*" Job 25:4 asks:

"How then can man be righteous *(tsadaq)* before God?

Or how can he be pure *(zakah)* who is born of a woman?"

Psalm 51:4 reads:

"Against thee, thee only, have I sinned, and done this evil in thy sight: that thou mightest be justified *(tsadaq)* when thou speakest, and be clear *(zakah)* when thou judgest" (KJV). (The NKJV has "blameless" in the place of "clear.")

Again, we see that the meaning of *tsadaq* is close enough to the idea of "cleanse" that the biblical writer can use it in a position of synonymous parallelism with *zakah,* a word meaning "clean" or "pure."

The KJV translates the Hebrew *tahor* 50 times as "clean," 41 times as "pure," twice as "fair," and once as "pureness." The version has rendered the Hebrew *zakah* twice as "be clean," twice as "cleanse," twice as "make clean," once as "clear," and once as "count pure."

Given these examples of close association between *tsadaq* and other Hebrew words that have as their primary meaning "clean," it is reasonable to state that the translation "cleansed" in Daniel 8:14 (KJV), though perhaps not the primary meaning of *tsadaq,* is certainly not an untenable rendering, not an overreach, nor far from the meaning incorporated within the word. We also see that because the biblical writer employs *tsadaq* in a position of synonymous parallelism with *tahor,* a word used to describe the function of Yom Kippur in Leviticus 16, the concept of Daniel 8:14 being somehow related to the Day of Atonement service is not an unreasonable one.

The Legal Connotation of *Tsadaq* ("Cleansed")

Let's now turn our attention to those texts that have a distinctly legal flavor to them. Although it could be argued that a large percentage of the 41 times that *tsadaq* appears, the word conveys a forensic overtone, we will take a closer look at a representative number of the passages.

Job 13:18

Job 13:18 says: "Behold now, I have ordered my cause; I know that I shall be justified *(tsadaq)*" (KJV).

The word "cause" ties directly to a litigation context. It means "case," or "suit," as in "lawsuit." The NKJV has: "See now, I have prepared my case, I know that I shall be vindicated *(tsadaq)*."

I would suppose that if the Bible had no other texts to support the Seventh-day Adventist interpretation of Daniel 8:14 and the pre-Advent judgment, this one text in Job 13:18 would suffice. It breathes a courtroom atmosphere and anticipates judicial proceedings that will result in exoneration. If the book of Job uses *tsadaq* to depict such a scene (a courtroom convening with vindication as its goal), why then would *tsadaq* in Daniel 8:14 not convey precisely the same meaning and force?

Isaiah 43:26

In Isaiah 43:26 we again see a distinctly legal flavor attending *tsadaq:* "Put Me in remembrance; let us contend together; state your case, that you may be acquitted *(tsadaq)*."

Is not the clear meaning of *tsadaq* in this verse one of court language involving the presentation of the case and a looking toward acquittal, the very essence of what Seventh-day Adventists believe Daniel 8:14 is referring to? If *tsadaq* can dress up in court clothes in Isaiah, why not also in Daniel?

Genesis 38:26

Genesis 38 recounts the story of Judah's sad affair with Tamar (her name means "palm"). Tamar had married Er, Judah's first-born, whose life was so wicked that "the Lord killed him" (Gen. 38:7). In keeping with the law of levirate marriages, it became incumbent upon Onan, the next of kin, to raise up a family in the name of his late brother by having children through Tamar. In this he failed and was also struck dead (verse 10).

Given the circumstances, Judah was no doubt reluctant to see all three of his sons predecease him, and so he held back from giving Shelah, his thirdborn, to Tamar. The life expectancy of her husbands wasn't too good, after all. At first Judah claimed that Shelah was too young, but as time went by, and Judah delayed, Tamar decided to take things into her own hands and force the issue. Evidently she was unhappy in her widowhood and impatient with her father-in-law. Disguising herself so that he wouldn't recognize her, she sat by the side of a road that she knew Judah would be traveling on his way to shear his sheep.

Thinking she was a prostitute and not realizing she was his daughter-in-law because she was veiled, Judah had relations with her, but because he could not pay her immediately, Tamar retained some personal items from him as a pledge. Later when Judah sent his servants to remunerate her and retrieve his "signature" seal and walking staff, the roadside harlot had disappeared and was nowhere to be found, nor did anyone there seem to know who she might have been. The frustrated servants returned home without the items held as a pledge.

Later Judah learned that Tamar had become pregnant. Thinking she was with child by harlotry, he ordered her death. "Bring her out and let her be burned!" he said (verse 24). One can only wonder if Judah was completely oblivious to his own misconduct—his conscience shielded by a chauvinistic double standard—or if his summary judgment resulted from a conscience smarting with guilt. (Sometimes we see our sins clearest when reflected in the conduct of others and are quick to judge the "mote" while our vision is obscured by a "beam"!)

His decision had the same force as a court in session. There may not have been a gavel or a bench, but judgment was in the air. Pregnant Tamar's life hung in the balance, and Judah was prepared to pass sentence against her. Then the accused daughter-in-law brought forth as evidence the personal items she had retained—Judah's signet and staff—that *he* had pledged on the occasion when *he* had caused her to be with child, not recognizing her as the one he had promised to Shelah.

Her life at stake, Tamar implored, "Please determine whose these are—the signet and cord, and staff" (verse 25). Chagrined, Judah had to acknowledge them as his own. Only then, when faced with such indisputable evidence, did Judah own up to his own misdeed. "She has been more righteous *(tsadaq)* than I" was his verdict (verse 26), and Tamar was vindicated and her life saved.

Perhaps we can step back for a moment and look at this story from a wider perspective. Tamar, the woman, could represent the church under a death sentence, the charges brought by an accuser who himself had played a major part in its predicament. "She was unfaithful; let her be burned," is the devil's closing argument against God's people, though he has repeatedly had a part in their transgression. But then evidence is submitted on the church's behalf, evidence that is not its own, but that serves to gain its acquittal *(tsadaq)*. This verdict of "not guilty" in the story of Tamar is exactly the message of the apocalyptic visions of Daniel ("judgment was made in favor of the saints of the Most High" [Dan. 7:22]) and the consequence of the cleansing of the sanctuary predicted in Daniel 8:14. Through the ministry of the heavenly sanctuary Christ procures for His church acquittal from sin's death decree.

Psalm 82:1-3

Some editions of the NKJV subtitle Psalm 82 as "A Plea for Justice." The psalm opens with the words "God stands in the congregation of the mighty; He judges among the gods [footnote: "gods"—the Hebrew word *elohim* means literally "powerful ones," that is the judges. Although most often applied to God, it is sometimes used in reference to humans in positions of authority]. How long will you judge unjustly, and show partiality to the wicked? . . . Defend the poor and fatherless; do justice *(tsadaq)* to the afflicted and needy" (Ps. 82:1-3).

Without question the context of the psalm has to do with the courtroom. Asaph is petitioning the judiciary of his day to dispense impartial justice, to render fair verdicts, and to uphold the cause of those less fortunate, a frequent theme in the Old Testament. Again, the distinct legal flavor of tsadaq is unmistakable, as is also the case in Job 34:5; Job 40:8; Psalm 143:2; and Isaiah 50:8.

Deuteronomy 25:1

Perhaps the clearest passage of all indicating the forensic posture of *tsadaq* is Moses' admonition in Deuteronomy 25:1. If it were the only other occurrence of *tsadaq,* and we had no lexicon or dictionary to help us define the word, this passage alone would provide us a clear understanding of what the verb is about. "If there is a dispute between men, and they come to court, that the judges may judge them, and they justify *(tsadaq)* the righteous and condemn the wicked . . ."

This text puts *tsadaq* squarely in the middle of the courtroom. It most certainly places the word in a legal environment involving a contested issue, witnesses to be heard, evidence to be weighed, a decision to be made, and a verdict to be pronounced. If the word *tsadaq* can wield a figurative gavel in Deuteronomy 25, we Seventh-day Adventists strongly suggest that it carries the same meaning with it to Daniel 8. What Adventists have taught regarding Daniel 8:14, the investigative judgment, and the word "cleansed" in that verse, as well as the proposition that the sanctuary being "cleansed" is an alternative expression for the court scene of Daniel 7 that culminates in judgment being pronounced in favor of the saints, thus stands on firm ground when we compare it to the usages of that word in other parts of the Bible.

Genesis 44:16

Joseph's brothers were in a quandary. After leaving Egypt in such high spirits and having enjoyed the hospitality of the prime minister himself, they now found themselves overtaken by his servants and accused of having taken the royal silver drinking cup. They made the sad return trip to Egypt and got hustled back to Joseph's house, where Judah spoke for the brothers in a heart-wrenching appeal to the prime minister (his own brother Joseph, though at that time he didn't realize it): "Then Judah said, 'What shall we say to my lord? What shall we speak? Or how shall we clear ourselves *(tsadaq)*'" (Gen. 44:16).

Again, we could make a strong argument that if we had no other sources to rely on but this passage, as far as understanding the picture that *tsadaq* conveys, this one text would go a long way toward building our understanding of the word's broad meaning. Exactly what did Judah mean when he used *tsadaq*? Did he not acknowledge that a charge had been made against him? Does not the context demand that the word looks forward to an opportunity to remove that indictment? Didn't Judah employ that word to anticipate a favorable verdict, an exoneration, a vindication? Wasn't he saying, "How can we be relieved of the burden of this charge and be declared innocent?" What other possible meaning can *tsadaq* have in this story? Who would argue that this isn't the clear meaning of *tsadaq* in Genesis 44? If that is the meaning of the word here, then it must also be the same in Daniel 8.

The investigative judgment as held by Seventh-day Adventists recognizes that Satan has brought charges against God and His people, and the express purpose of this judicial process is to clear the names of those involved, to remove the burden of the indictments and achieve vindication, as depicted in the judicial picture of Daniel 7. The usages of *tsadaq* in texts such as Genesis 44 support the Adventist position.

2 Samuel 15:4

The last example of *tsadaq* that we'll highlight occurs in the tragic story of Absalom. Talented and charming, Absalom became infatuated by his own appearance and like Lucifer, another King's son before him, ambitiously sought to wrest the throne from his father. Instead of launching an open attack against David's regime, Absalom went behind his father's back and initiated a whispering campaign by which he effectively "stole the hearts of the men of Israel" (2 Sam. 15:6). As you read the following passage, remember that in Old Testament times the gate was the place to administer judgment (see, for example, Deuteronomy 16:18; 21:19; 22:15; 25:7; Joshua 20:4; Ruth 4:1; Daniel 2:49; Zechariah 8:16; etc.):

"Now Absalom would rise early and stand beside the way to the gate. So it was, whenever anyone who had a lawsuit came to the king for a decision, that Absalom would call to him and say, 'What city are you from?' And he would say, 'Your servant is from such and such a tribe of Israel.' Then Absalom would say to him, 'Look, your case is good and right; but there is no deputy of the king to hear you.' Moreover Absalom would say, 'Oh, that I were made judge in the land, and everyone who has any suit or cause would come to me; then I would give him justice *(tsadaq)*'" (2 Sam. 15:2-4).

Unfortunately, Absalom, the one whose name means "the father of peace," became "the father of tumult," the disseminator of discontent, the instigator of civil conflict, a pattern hearkening back to that war that broke out in heaven as a result of the unrest instigated by Lucifer.

What meaning does *tsadaq* convey in this story? Clearly it occurs in the setting of litigation. Isn't Absalom proposing to hear the cases brought to him, to listen as the witnesses give their testimony, to sift through the evidence offered, to decide which case has merit and which does not, and then to pronounce a verdict that will mean victory for one party and defeat for the other? Only a severe case of biased myopia would cause one to deny the legal flavor of *tsadaq* in the story of Absalom. If that is what the word meant in David's day, then surely it had the same aspect in Daniel's time. The connotation of *tsadaq* in 2 Samuel 15 can reasonably transfer to Daniel 8:14, solidifying the Seventh-day Adventist teaching of the investigative judgment.

Word Study Summary

In summary, we have seen that Scripture frequently uses *tsadaq* synonymously with words such as "clean," "pure," and "clear," leading us to believe that the translation "cleansed" does not violate the word's inherent meaning. Specifically, we have seen it used in synonymous parallelism with the word *tahor,* which Leviticus 16 employs to define the objective of the Day of Atonement service. The rendition "cleansed" has merit not only because Scripture closely associates *tsadaq* with other Hebrews words meaning "cleansed," but because it can also be understood in a forensic sense, as having one's record "cleansed," "cleared," or "expunged," the outgrowth of the legal process of vindication or exoneration.

In conjunction with that concept, we have repeatedly observed *tsadaq* within a setting of litigation. It frequently appears in the framework of the "gate," or court. Thus, an examination of the contexts in which it appears provides a compelling reason for concluding that the word *tsadaq* indeed comes dressed in legal garb. Just to see that word in Daniel 8:14 would naturally lead one to expect a courtroom atmosphere of cases heard, testimony introduced, evidence presented, decisions rendered, and verdicts implemented.

Since the visions of Daniel 7 and 8 have so much in common, and because the cleansing of the sanctuary functions as the pivotal point of the passage in Daniel 8, resulting in the turning of the tide from evil's having the upper hand to evil's being put down (just as the court scene of Daniel 7 is the fulcrum of that vision), and given the forensic connotation of *tsadaq,* it is entirely reasonable to look upon Daniel 8:14 as somehow reflecting Daniel 7:9, 10; to view the court scene of Daniel 7 as somehow being connected with the cleansing of the sanctuary of Daniel 8. The Seventh-day Adventist view that Daniel 8:14 portrays a heavenly tribunal and reflects the court scene of Daniel 7:9,10 is a well-justified conclusion based on a study of *tsadaq* in other verses.

Daniel 8:14 predicts that something of a judicial nature will take place. Why does Scripture place it in the context of the sanctuary? And why does the passage employ sanctuary terminology? Because, as we've seen, the vision of chapter 8 is set in an overall sanctuary context. What in the sanctuary service was most closely associated with judgment? Yom Kippur, the Day of Atonement service, a fact still reflected clearly in Jewish literature. Why do Seventh-day Adventists look at Daniel 8:14 as referring to the sanctuary in heaven? Because the fulfillment of this 2300-day/year prophecy occurs at a time when the *earthly* sanctuary no longer exists, and because the earthly sanctuary was only a type, or shadow, of the original in heaven in the first place (Heb. 8:5).

As for the translations of other versions, Adventists surely have nothing to fear from the rendition "justified," "purified," or "put right" as long as we recognize the whole flavor of *tsadaq.* Court proceedings result in defendants' being justified, or declared innocent, or vindicated, or having their record purged of charges made against it. It is through the judicial process that one's standing and record get put right.

The NIV's "reconsecrated" and the RSV's "restored to its rightful state" are more unfortunate than wrong, in that they seem to place the emphasis of the prophecy on a physical rebuilding of the Temple, a concept borne out not nearly as clearly by the usages of *tsadaq* in other passages as is the "courtroom acquittal" motif. In addition, no one has ever demonstrated a logical, accurate explanation of how the physical rebuilding of the Temple would have been fulfilled historically according to a 2300-day/year time line.

Chapter Five

Narrative Study

Biblical narratives are an excellent source for the study of theological teaching. Theology, in its purest form, is understanding what kind of a being God is and how He relates to His creatures. Better than mere words or sentences, with their restricted definitions and limited contexts, a story is a living illustration of God in action. In His supreme revelation of Himself, God sent us His Son to live out His doctrine. The greatest theological documents ever given are a crib and a cross. All the words, sermons, epistles, and scholarly apologies ever written could never come close to matching the message of who God is and what He is like that we find conveyed in the stories of Bethlehem and Calvary. Up to this point our study has focused primarily on words and linguistics. In the narrative portion we will concentrate more on the concept of the pre-Advent judgment.

What do the stories of the Bible say with regard to God's pattern of dealing with His sinful creatures? Can we detect any trend in how He relates to those who have disobeyed Him? Specifically, is it possible to see the last-day worldwide investigative judgment mirrored in God's activity toward transgressors on a smaller scale?

Adam and Eve and the Investigative Judgment

Let's begin by looking at the story contained in Genesis 3, that of the unhappy fall from innocence of our first parents. It is the first illustration of God's dealing with sinful human behavior, and usually the initial example given in the Bible for anything deserves careful scrutiny and serves as a model for future incidents.

After Adam and Eve had both eaten the forbidden fruit, Scripture tells us that God came looking for them in the "cool of the day" (Gen. 3:8). When the Lord found them, Adam explained that they had hidden themselves because of their shame. The Lord then inquired, "Who told you that you were naked? Have you eaten from the tree of which I commanded you that you should not eat?'" (verse 11).

Reflect on this conversation for just a moment. God called out "Where are you?" and "Have you eaten of the forbidden tree?" Without sounding facetious, we wonder: Did God ask those questions because He was ignorant? Did He really not know where Adam and Eve were when He came to Eden? Was He really not aware that they had eaten the proscribed fruit? To accept those notions as true would be to reject the clear Bible teaching of God's omniscience. As we've noted, the Bible states unequivocally that God knows everything. So we must conclude that when He questioned Adam and Eve, it wasn't because He didn't already know, but for a different reason.

Within a short time the Lord would have to drive out the errant couple from the garden, separating them from the tree whose fruit perpetuated life—and more important, from His visible and unrestricted presence. He would pronounce a series of curses, the first against the serpent, restricting it to traveling on the ground; the second against the woman, placing her in a position subservient to her husband and making the act of childbirth a painful one; and the third against Adam, making the process of earning a living a difficult and arduous one. Finally, He declared that their lives would end in the grave.

Although the language seems harsh, their sentence was in fact far more lenient than they deserved. Earlier God had plainly told them that death—the kind that the Bible calls the "second," or "eternal," death—would be the result of disobedience. But in mercy He was allowing them another chance. However, they would have to leave their Eden home and face the consequences of their disloyalty.

But before implementing such far-reaching judgments, God condescended to look personally into the behavior of His creatures—to investigate by questioning them. This was not because He didn't already know where they were and what they had done, but to give them confidence that His forthcoming judgments were fair and based on accurate knowledge. God had every right to remove them from the garden without any further explanation. Nothing demanded that He come to them personally, nor was He obliged to speak to them at all. They had disobeyed and deserved the consequences of their transgression without any additional explanation.

But He didn't take this approach. Instead, He personally visited the garden, and He employed language that would increase their appreciation of His justice in rendering His verdict. The issue of God's fairness is central to the battle between God and Satan, and so God traveled the extra mile, doing that which He is not required to do, to inspire in His subjects an appreciation for the fact that He is not arbitrary in His dealings with humanity. He *investigates before He acts.*

I well remember those occasions as a youngster when my misbehavior earned me paternal discipline. Even today I still vividly recall that my dad would go over the misdeed (calmly, I might add) and make sure I understood what it was I had done wrong. Next (for me as a disobedient child, the hardest part) we had prayer about the matter. Then he would administer the "board of education" to the "seat of understanding," accompanied appropriately by my loud and lusty lamentations. Though these moments were not frequent (I heard about a family that had a wall-mounted leather razor strop reserved for such purposes, above which hung the inscription "I need thee every hour"!) and never welcome, in time I came to believe that my father did everything in love, not revenge, and that he meant it to be truly "disciplinary," that is, a learning experience. I remember that there was an inquiry before the punishment, just as in the story of Adam and Eve and the first sin.

Genesis 3 and its description of God's coming to this earth also points to the last days and serves as a type of Christ's second coming. "For whatever things were written before were written for our learning, that we through the patience and comfort of the

Scriptures might have hope" (Rom. 15:4).

"Now all these things happened to them as examples, and they were written for our admonition, upon whom the ends of the ages have come" (1 Cor. 10:11).

When Jesus comes back, unrepentant sinners will flee from His presence, just as the first sinners did. In God's presence they will realize, maybe for the first time, the shame of their true condition of moral nakedness, and they will try by any means to run and hide. While the righteous rise to meet Him in the sky, sinners will gnash their teeth and long for the grave to ease the pain of a tortured conscience.

But before God takes action against those who have rejected His grace, He will conduct a divine inquiry into each case, not because He does not know the just reward of every person, but to inspire in the hearts of those who are not omniscient, as He is, that He operates from a position of knowledge and fairness. If God dealt with sin that way at its inception, would we not expect Him to do the same at its conclusion?

Cain and the Investigative Judgment

We might title Genesis 3, the story of Adam and Eve, "The Forbidden Fruit." In one sense Genesis 4, the story of Cain's rejected fruit offering, might be entitled "The Forbidden Fruit, Part 2." How did God deal with Cain's murder of his brother?

As He did with Adam and Eve after their sin, we find the Lord also seeking out Cain and asking questions about his conduct before pronouncing judgment against him. "Then the Lord said to Cain, 'Where is Abel your brother?' He said, 'I do not know. Am I my brother's keeper?' And He said, 'What have you done? The voice of your brother's blood cries out to me from the ground'" (Gen. 4:9, 10). God then invoked a curse on Cain's ability to farm the land and placed a mark on Cain so that no one would take his life in revenge.

Again we might ask, Didn't God know what had happened between Cain and Abel? Didn't He know that Cain had murdered his brother? And didn't He know where Abel's body lay? To each question we have to say, Of course He knew. But before pronouncing judgment against Cain, He investigated the circumstances of Cain's conduct. He did it, not because legally required to do so, but so that, by lowering Himself to speak in human terms, Cain might know that the judgment he was to receive was fair and just. *Once again, before God took action, He investigated.*

As with the story of Adam and Eve, this incident also teaches us about the last days, at which time, according to the prophecies of Revelation, worship will again be at issue. Remember that both brothers worshiped, but because of Abel's faithfulness God accepted his sacrifice while rejecting Cain's. The rejection incited his sibling's jealous and violent rage, resulting in Abel's death. After Cain's heinous crime God looked into the matter and placed a mark on him so that no one might take his life in vengeance. Cain was protected, while Abel was martyred.

The story of Cain and Abel is Revelation 13 in reverse. At the end of time God will have people who will be faithful to Him in the matter of worship, keeping His seventh-day Sabbath holy according to the commandment. They will choose to worship Him who "made heaven and earth" (Rev. 14:7) rather than the beast and his image (Rev. 13:15). Satan will instigate great envy against them and will seek to destroy them. However, in *contrast* to the story of Cain and Abel, at the end of this earth's history God will intervene and place His seal of protection on those who honor Him, and they will not become martyrs as did Abel.

On the other hand, those intent on persecuting His chosen ones will receive the mark of the beast but not the benefit of God's protection. Why the contrast, you might ask? Why was Abel not shielded, but Cain spared? It is because in the Genesis account the drama of human sin was in its early chapters. The story was just unfolding. God protected Cain for the same reason that He did not immediately snuff Lucifer and his angels out when war broke out in heaven. The full effects of rebellion against God had not yet been fully exposed, nor could they be fully understood. For this reason, as the conflict moved to our planet and its inhabitants, God must not intervene every time He would like to (though He surely would have desired to prevent the murder of His obedient son, Abel), for that would not allow the seeds of sin to germinate and sprout into the evil plant that it is, bringing forth its noxious fruit. Unfortunately, the whole universe must know what the final results of sin are.

Where we live, Bermuda grass, similar to crabgrass, grows abundantly. It's a continuing battle to try to control it in those areas that I'd like to reserve for gardening. What I've learned is that a product called Roundup does quite well, but it does no good to spray it until the blades have grown sufficiently to absorb the herbicide. The chemicals will then travel to the root of the weed. In fact, the directions suggest that (if it's a Bermuda grass or crabgrass lawn you're dealing with) you skip your last mowing so that the spray will receive maximum absorption. In a similar way, the "Cains" of this world must have enough latitude to "leaf out" and demonstrate the fruitage of wickedness.

Conversely, as the story of sin approaches its final chapter all will have witnessed the results of sin. An Everest of convincing and unmistakable evidence will support the conclusion that rebellion against God wreaks nothing but woe, sorrow, pain, and death.

After human probation has closed, it will no longer serve any purpose for the latter-day Cains to work out their murderous vengeance against their brothers. Throughout human history the blood of the martyrs has been the seed of the gospel. Conversions have resulted when sinners such as Saul have witnessed the final end of saints such as Stephen, who have signed their testimony in blood. Impressed by what they have seen on the faces of the faithful, many have accepted Christ. (The primary meaning of the Greek word "martyr" is "witness.") But after probation has closed, every mind will have already made its ultimate decision. Everyone will have sealed their destiny for eternity, and Jesus' pronouncement "He who is holy, let him be holy still" (Rev. 22:11) will have been enacted. Because the death of His children would no longer serve any useful purpose, it will be God's pleasure to graciously cover His faithful with His feathers and give them refuge beneath His wings. Then we will see fulfilled the psalm that promises: "A thousand may fall at your side, and ten thousand at your right hand; but it shall not come near you. Only with your eyes shall you look, and see the reward of the wicked. Because you have made the Lord, who is my refuge, even the Most High, your dwelling place, no evil shall befall you, nor shall any plague come near your dwelling" (Ps. 91:7-10).

For the same reason, there will be no need to provide special protection for the Cains of the last day. Whereas God marked for protection the first son to be born on the earth, and gave him time to develop fully and expose his character clearly, allowing the universe to see sin in its true light, the last-day rebels will have characters that demonstrate a completely matured evil. Moreover, the record book of earth's legacy of sin will have been baptized in the blood of the righteous and will be spilling over with evidence as to the conduct of evildoers. Therefore, they will receive no mark of protection to spare them from the effects of the seven last plagues or the self-destructive violence that will descend upon the earth following the withdrawal of God's gracious Spirit from those who have ultimately turned their backs on Him.

But as in the case of Cain, a divine inquiry into humanity's activities will take place prior to the implementation of the divine verdict—not because God is ignorant about human sins, but to nourish the confidence of those who can't read minds and hearts, as He can. It will assure them that His judgment is fair and just. *Before God takes action, He always investigates.* God greatly desires for His creatures to be convinced, not beyond a reasonable doubt (the test for juries in the criminal courts of our land today), but beyond the shadow of a doubt, as to His fairness in His dealings with each individual.

The Flood and the Investigative Judgment

"As the days of Noah were, so also will the coming of the Son of Man be" (Matt. 24:37).

What can we learn about the investigative judgment from the story of the Flood? We know that it illustrates last-day events. Does anything in the account shed light on the topic we're examining? Two things emerge that bear on our study. First, that God *looked* before He acted, and second, that the decisions of all, both those inside the ark and out, were *finalized* and *recognized* for a period of time before the Flood took place.

"Then the Lord saw that the wickedness of man was great in the earth, and that every intent of the thoughts of his heart was only evil continually" (Gen. 6:5).

It is interesting that the text doesn't say "And God, *knowing* that man was wicked . . ." Unlike most New Testament verbs translated "to see," which have at their root the concept of "to know," the Hebrew *ra'ah* means primarily "to see," "to look," "to consider," and "to behold." God *looked* before He announced and set in motion His judgment against the earth. But He didn't have to. His divine wisdom didn't require it, but nevertheless the record states that He took a visual inventory of conditions on earth prior to sending His judgment against it. *He investigated before He took action.* If this was God's method of dealing with sin prior to the earth's first destruction, would we expect it to be any different the next time?

We read that God commissioned Noah to build an ark and preach for 120 years something that seemed impossible. Never before had it rained on earth, and the prospect of a worldwide flood seemed ridiculous to the earth's pre-Flood population. When he and his sons had finally completed the vessel, Noah made one final appeal before he, his wife, and their three sons and wives went into the ark. Then the antediluvian menagerie marched up the gangplank, and God closed the door (Gen. 7:16). Those on the ark said goodbye to a world that would look dramatically different when they disembarked more than a year later.

Then there followed a period of seven days that might have seemed like seven years to those inside the ark. At first nothing happened. Through the window of the ark they could see day after day the same clear sky as always. Some of their neighbors likely went back to work on that new house they were building. Others were engrossed in the plans for an upcoming wedding. Many returned their hand to the plow or the saw. During the first few days after God shut the door of the ark, life went on as it always had.

No doubt some of their critics made fun of what they considered Noah's madness. Crowds of neighbors and relatives gathered outside, mocking, taunting, and jeering. "Come out, old man," they must have scorned. The impressive sight of the arrival of the animals and the closing of the mighty door quickly faded in the bright sunshine of cloudless skies during the days immediately following Noah's entry.

It must have put his faith to a severe test. Had he indeed followed God's counsel? Was all his talk of a flood just a mirage? How long should they wait in the ark before reconsidering? The devil must have assailed him with doubts about his faith.

But on the seventh day it was different. On that day the blue sky became gray as clouds covered it. When the first drops began to fall, fear seized the hearts of those antediluvian infidels as they now began to realize their worst nightmare. Despite what all the philosophers, scientists, scholars, and pundits had told them, Noah was right. And now he was in the boat while they were on the outside. They could easily have been inside with Noah. After all, how much physical effort would it have required to walk up that gangplank? But their disbelieving and foolish pride had stopped them, and without exception those on the outside were all eventually swept to destruction.

God is not arbitrary. His judgments are just. The Flood narrative reveals that each person had a choice about whether to be in the ark or not—to be saved or lost. They could exhibit that choice by the physical act of boarding the vessel, something that each person there could have done. And so it is with salvation. God offers it to everyone. Christ's death on the cross provided the means for each person on earth to be saved, but God leaves it with the individual to make their decision about whether or not to accept the gift of eternal life.

The story further illustrates that there came a time when all decisions were finalized, and everyone who would be in the boat was inside, and all those who rejected the offer of salvation were outside. Ultimately God recognized that each person had exercised their final choice, and He solemnized that moment of destiny by closing the ark's door, an act that corresponded to the "shutting of the gates" of Yom Kippur in Jewish theology. "The Lord shut him in" (Gen. 7:16). But the rain did not start instantly with the closing of the door, nor did destruction immediately accompany the sealing of Noah's ship of salvation. No, following this finalization of all decisions, there occurred a period of time (seven days) before the salvation/destruction event unfolded.

By the same token, at the end of the age but prior to the return of Christ to earth there will come a time when every person will have made their final decision, and God will close the door of salvation. The judgment isn't so much God's deciding who is going to be saved and who is going to be lost as it is His recognizing our decision as to whether we choose to accept His provision to be saved or decide that we would rather be lost. The lost in Noah's day decided of their own volition to remain outside the ark of salvation.

Likewise, at the end of earth's history there will be a period (no doubt a short one) between the time when the door of mercy is shut, closing probation for the human family, and when the salvation/destruction event takes place. We see this fixing of all destinies *prior to* the Advent in a statement Jesus made:

"He who is unjust, let him be unjust still; he who is filthy, let him be filthy still; he who is righteous, let him be righteous still; he who is holy, let him be holy still. And behold, I am coming quickly, and My reward is with Me, to give to everyone according to his work" (Rev. 22:11, 12).

During this period the righteous will find their faith challenged, just as was that of Noah and his family. The adage says "Character is not made in a crisis. It is only exhibited." This will be a time in which character will be on display, both for the saved and unsaved. The fruitage of character, either mature in righteousness or ripe in wickedness, will be fully exposed for all the universe to see. Spiritual polarization will have taken place, with each person either filled entirely with God's Spirit or completely devoid of His gracious presence.

The Tower of Babel and the Investigative Judgment

Regrettably, it took but a relatively short time following the Deluge before humanity became immersed in iniquity once more. Shrugging off the promise that God would not again destroy the world with a flood, they purposed to build a tower to heaven that would protect them from a future inundation, and at the same time be a monument to their ingenuity. They exhibited their rejection of God's will by clustering in a few cities rather than spreading out to repopulate the earth as the Lord desired. "Come, let us build ourselves a city, and a tower whose top is in the heavens; let us make a name for ourselves, lest we be scattered abroad over the face of the whole earth" (Gen. 11:4).

The Hebrews associated the name of the tower—Babel—with the similar-sounding Hebrew word for "confusion," reflecting the initiation of different languages, which became a part of the story. But to the later dwellers of Shinar, Babel became the root for the name Babylon, translated as "gate of the gods," and revealed the blasphemous intent of the architects of this project "whose top is in the heavens." It echoed the attitude of Lucifer, the originator of sin, who sought to "ascend into heaven" and exalt his "throne above the stars of God" (Isa. 14:13).

Their tower was an act of defiance against God, and it met with His disapproval. But before He would summarily execute His judgment against them, He announced that He would personally inspect their conduct. "The Lord came down to see the city and the tower which the sons of men had built" (Gen. 11:5). We ask, Is it possible that God didn't know what was going on with Babel's builders? Was the Lord off on another project in the universe so that what these rebels were doing had escaped His attention? Surely He knew fully not only their acts but also their hearts. And yet Scripture tells us that He "came down to see" what was going on! *As always, He investigated before He took action.* Was it necessary for Him to "come down and see" in order to fulfill the requirements of divine justice? Not at all. In His omniscience He could have taken action against them without having gone the extra mile to "come down and see." But that is consistently how the Bible presents the pattern of God's dealings with His errant creatures. The "coming down" represents His condescending nature, ultimately reaching its climax in the birth of Jesus, the God-man. It seems that He is always "coming down" to our level to explain things in a way that we might comprehend. If He looked to see what transgressors were doing at Babel, how much more does it make sense that He would also investigate before taking action against a worldwide last-day Babel?

Sodom and Gomorrah and the Investigative Judgment

"As it was in the days of Lot . . . even thus shall it be in the day when the Son of man is revealed" (Luke 17:28-30, KJV).

Genesis 19 records the distressing account of the final end of the "cities of the plain," including Sodom and Gomorrah. When the time had come for Abram and his nephew to part company, Lot set his gaze toward the Dead Sea valley. "And Lot lifted his eyes and saw all the plain of Jordan, that it was well watered everywhere (before the Lord destroyed Sodom and Gomorrah) like the garden of the Lord, like the land of Egypt as you go toward Zoar" (Gen. 13:10).

Lured by Sodom's charms, Lot had at first "pitched his tent toward Sodom" (verse 12, KJV), but eventually its seductive magnetism had drawn him into its evil vortex. By the time the Lord took action against the city, Lot found himself not just a sojourner in Sodom but no doubt a leading citizen (Gen. 19:1). (In Old Testament times, to "sit at the gate" indicated a position or role of decision-making, and this verse was perhaps the root of the allusion in Genesis 19:9), though it seems that Lot had had some second thoughts about making his home there. Peter says that the evils of Sodom "vexed his righteous soul" (2 Peter 2:8, KJV).

How tragic that within just a few centuries following the Flood, evil had again flourished to the magnitude that it took drastic and decisive action to stem the tide. It is instructive to note that the sins that plagued Sodom and Gomorrah are the hallmark of our own age. Indeed, the evangelist Billy Graham is credited with stating something to the effect that if the Lord doesn't come soon, He's going to have to apologize to Sodom and Gomorrah. We usually think of the wickedness of Sodom and Gomorrah in terms of immorality, and it's true that such sins were both present and blatant. But Ezekiel opens our eyes to other types of wickedness that permeated these cities of the past:

"Look, this was the iniquity of your sister Sodom: She and her daughter had pride, fullness of food, and abundance of idleness; neither did she strengthen the hand of the poor and needy. And they were haughty and committed abomination before Me; therefore I took them away as I saw fit" (Eze. 16:49, 50).

Before destroying the cities of the plain, the Lord paid a visit to His friend Abraham. One day as the patriarch was relaxing in the shade of a terebinth grove, he noticed three strangers approaching. Exhibiting true Middle Eastern hospitality, the patriarch urged them to stop at his home for some refreshment before continuing on their way. Clearly Abraham had no clue as to the real identity of his guests, and the writer of Hebrews no doubt refers to this experience in remarking that some have entertained angels "unawares" (Heb. 13:2, KJV).

One wonders whether the patriarch later reflected on the day's events and was grateful that kindness was in his heart when they approached! One wonders what the outcome might have been, and how the story might have changed (remember that the visit not only concerned the destruction of the evil cities but also the birth of Isaac: it was a life-*and*-death matter), had Abraham not invited them to his home. How much he would have missed!

After honoring Abraham by eating the meal prepared for them, and after reemphasizing the promise that Sarah would bear a son, one of the guests (whom Abraham now knew to be the Lord) turned His attention to the second half of His mission. "And the Lord said, 'Because the outcry against Sodom and Gomorrah is great, and because their sin is very grave, *I will go down now and see* whether they have done altogether according to the outcry against it that has come to Me; and if not, I will know'" (Gen. 18:20, 21).

Again, we must deal with the question: If the Lord is omniscient (and He *is*), and if He knows everything (and He *does*), what can this statement possibly mean? Can it possibly be true that

God wasn't already fully aware of the moral pigsty represented by those cities? That He didn't know that they had filled their cup of iniquity to overflowing? Of course not! The Lord most certainly had a complete grasp of the wickedness in those cities. Nothing can escape His attention. Those things thought to be done in secret are as visible to His eyes as if they had happened in the open. And yet He said, "I will look and then I will know."

Why then did the Lord make such a statement to Abraham? Again, it is because it is His pattern to speak in language that His subjects understand, in order to give them confidence that He is fair in His judgments. The phrase "I will go down" is a window into God's condescending character.

Notice three ways that God stooped to meet Abraham on his level: Appearing on a dusty road as a weary traveler, the Lord first condescended to *approach* Abraham in a way that would make him comfortable with His presence. Second, He *ate* his food in a way that would make Abraham feel at ease. It's a worldwide law of human nature that to accept food from another is a shortcut in building relationships. One might inquire: Were the Lord and His companions really hungry that day? Had the angelic supply of food run short? No! But imagine the feeling that Abraham could cherish for the rest of his lifetime: "He ate at my table." The Lord didn't need to eat, but He did anyway. He went beyond what was necessary. And third, God *spoke* to him in a way that would make Abraham feel confident that God was trustworthy and that He made His decisions on a level of fairness born of knowledge. Nothing required God to do any of these things, but He did them to bring Abraham into a closer relationship with Him.

In the same way, at the end of time, before God rains fire and brimstone on the modern-day Sodoms and Gomorrahs, there will have been a divine inquiry, an investigative judgment, to double-check that they deserved their fate, not because God in His omniscience doesn't already know, but to give His creatures confidence that His verdicts are fair and that He pronounces them from a position of knowledge. The story of God and His destruction of the cities of the plain tells us clearly that *before He acts, He investigates.*

Joseph and the Investigative Judgment

The story of Joseph and his brothers mirrors many of the principles of the investigative judgment.

Because of the false charge levied by Potiphar's wife, Joseph's master threw him into prison, where he correctly interpreted the dreams of two of his fellow inmates, a butler, who was released, and a baker, who was executed. Following the butler's restoration, two full years passed, and Joseph's hopes that his former prison-mate would put in a good word for him evaporated like desert dew. Then Pharaoh himself had two dreams that neither he nor his counselors could decipher. Memories and promises that had lain dormant within the butler's mind began to surface, and he suggested that he knew someone who might be able to help. Summoned to Pharaoh's court, with God's help Joseph interpreted the two dreams—the heads of grain and the cows. Joseph forecast seven years of plenty followed by seven years of famine.

He advised that Pharaoh select someone to gather and bank the extra grain during the first seven years so that the nation would have a surplus to dispense during the looming famine. Without hesitation Pharaoh appointed Joseph to administer the task and conferred on him a title second only to his own. During the next seven years, when the "earth brought forth by handfuls" (Gen. 41:47, KJV), Joseph's crew collected and stored 20 percent of the harvest.

But then all too soon the seven years of plenty ended, and seven years of drought and famine followed. The people began looking to the Egyptian throne to provide for them. This was true not only in Egypt but also in the surrounding areas affected by the famine, including Canaan, where Jacob and his 11 sons lived.

Did Joseph wonder how long it would be before members of his family joined the long lines of Egyptians purchasing the grain he had collected and stored? Meanwhile he struggled with other questions—questions about his family. Was his father still living? And what about his siblings? If they did come to Egypt, would they be the same brothers who had so cruelly sold him into slavery? Maybe, as he saw the dominoes of circumstance falling, he anticipated their arrival and considered how he might determine the true nature of their hearts now, 20 years later.

When the brothers did reach Egypt, Joseph recognized them as they bowed before him. But the sons of Jacob did not know him. Their eyes saw only a distinguished Egyptian dignitary, one deserving the utmost honor and respect, as their lives were literally in his hands. After all, Joseph the prime minister looked and sounded different than the teenage brother they had sold in Dothan. His garb would have been the crisp Egyptian white loincloth of linen—washed and starched daily—rather than the rough shepherd dress of Hebrew nomads. His hair would have been shorter, and he would have been clean-shaven, in contrast to the longer hairstyles and bearded faces of the Hebrews. The language he spoke would have been to the brothers a foreign tongue. But more than this, there was the sheer improbability that this ruler could actually be their brother.

After a severe interrogation punctuated with accusations of espionage, Joseph put them all in prison for three days (to give them a brief introduction to Egyptian prisons?) with the proposal that one of the brothers remain as a hostage while the others returned to Canaan. They could come back to Egypt only if accompanied by the youngest brother, Benjamin (Joseph's only full brother), whose name had come up in conversation.

Joseph then initiated the first of his three tests. He would engineer a set of circumstances that would reveal where their hearts were. To accomplish this, Joseph instructed his servants to put the money that the brothers had paid for grain back in their sacks. Why did he do this? Undoubtedly it was an act of generosity toward his father. But it was much more than mere kindness, as admirable as that might have been.

What would their reaction be when they found their money returned in their sacks? Would greed control? Would they silently keep it and count it as a deserved windfall? The nine brothers had not gone far in their journey homeward when they discovered un-expected pieces of silver first in one sack and then another. (Our word "sack" is one of the few examples of words taken directly into our language from Hebrew *"saq".*) Afraid that it was an evil omen, they felt their spirits sink like a brick in the Nile, and like too many of us, they even resorted to blaming God for what had happened.

After many days of traveling the caravan reached the tent of Jacob and the sons reported all that had taken place, including the stipulation that Benjamin accompany them the next time they ran short and had to return to Egypt. Their stock of grain didn't last like the widow of Zarephath's flour, and so when the pur-chased provisions ran out and the inevitable time came, Judah pledged himself for Benjamin's safe return. Reluctantly Jacob sent his precious son into the dark uncertainty of that foreign land. To win the favor of the prime minister, they put together a sampler of choice local treats. Then Jacob ordered, "Take double money in your hand, and take back in your hand the money that was re-turned in the mouth of your sacks; perhaps it was an oversight" (Gen. 43:12).

When they returned to the land of the Nile, they received, to their surprise, an invitation to eat with the prime minister himself! As they tried to rectify the problem of the money that they had found in their grain sacks, they were pleased to hear the steward assure them, "Do not be afraid. Your God . . . has given you trea-sure in your sacks; I had your money" (verse 23). I am sure that Joseph noted the fact that they had brought the money back and had attempted to make things right.

Having obtained a favorable result to his first test, Joseph was ready to begin his second examination. To set the stage properly, he had the brothers seated around the dining table in the exact order of their ages, from oldest to youngest. We can only wonder how long it took for the sons of Israel (Jacob) to discern this odds-defying seating pattern. (Think of what the statistical odds would be to ar-range unknowingly 11 people by their correct ages. The mathemat-ical formula for that equation is $11 \times 10 \times 9 \times 8 \times 7 \times 6 \times 5 \times 4 \times 3 \times 2 \times 1$, coming out to 39,916,800. Call it one chance in 40 million if it were to happen by sheer coincidence!) Scripture states simply, "The men marvelled one at another" (Gen. 43:33, KJV).

Because Egyptians did not like to eat with Hebrews, Joseph played the role of an Egyptian and ate by himself. Without question, though, he was close enough to see and hear all that happened.

Egyptian royalty and nobility knew how to entertain. At a typical party the servant-to-guest ratio would have been one-to-one. Servants and guests alike would have worn on their heads cones of perfume that would melt during the festivity and spike the air with their pungent odors. Music would have come from an orchestra having 22-stringed harps, six-stringed lyres, three-stringed lutes, double reed pipes, and tambourines. Dancing girls and juggling men would have provided a visual spectacle. Bouquets of flowers would have adorned the room. The biblical account doesn't describe what accompanied Joseph's banquet, but we can guess that he did not spare any detail.

Soon delicious aromas filled the air as smartly attired waiters placed tray after tray of Egyptian delicacies, prepared by the prime minister's chef, before the widening eyes of the visiting brothers. Scripture doesn't tell us what was on the menu that day, but since it was a royal banquet, it might have included a salad course featuring lettuce, cucumbers, leeks, onions, and radishes; fruits such as dates, figs, pomegranates, melons, and grapes; vegetables served with an oil and vinegar dressing; peas and ful medames, a special dish prepared from ful, ancient Egyptian beans; fish caught by hook or harpoon from the Nile (although, since fish was generally considered a food for the poorer classes, it might not have qualified for this meal); breads and honey-sweetened pastries; roasted, boiled, or fried meats, such as domesticated sheep, goat, or ox, or perhaps deer or gazelle garnered by a royal hunting safari, foods that the poor seldom enjoyed, and that Egyptians reserved for very special occasions; and duck or geese from the papyrus marshes of the Nile, courtesy of one of Pharaoh's fowling expeditions. There might have been a famine in the land, but you wouldn't know it by the cornucopia on Joseph's table!

Since some of what they ate might be considered finger food, servants stood nearby, ready to offer bowls of scented water and freshly laundered linen napkins to wash and dry the hands. And through it all Joseph kept his eyes and ears open, primed to pick up crumbs of conversation, especially as servants heaped the plate of his only true brother, Benjamin, with five times the amount of food as that of any of the others. Joseph watched and wondered. Would he see a raised eyebrow of envy? Would there be a hushed, disparaging remark? Would there be a look of disdain toward Joseph's full brother? Were they the same brothers who had sold Joseph into slavery? In the 20 years that had passed, had the Spirit of God been able to work in their hearts to change their sinful and selfish characters? As his servants paraded in with the Egyptian delicacies in their respective courses, Joseph looked and listened with eager anticipation to discover the answers to his questions.

Apparently they were different now. Throughout the entire meal not a whisper of discontent shadowed the joy in the banquet hall, and so that night Joseph went to his quarters happy in the hope that his brothers had indeed changed. But the investigation had not yet concluded. The third test would be the hardest one of all. Joseph had designed one that would, to the best of his ability, re-create what had happened 20 years before in Dothan. Like the children of Israel later revisiting Kadesh Barnea before entering the Promised Land, the brothers would find themselves brought back precisely to the point at which they had sold Joseph into slavery. This examination would put the question squarely to them: Would they do the same today, if given the opportunity, as they did before? Would they be willing to sell a brother today if they had another chance?

To set up the situation, Joseph instructed his servants to place his own royal silver drinking cup in the sack belonging to Benjamin. "And he commanded the steward of his house, saying, 'Fill the men's sacks with food, as much as they can carry, and put each man's money in the mouth of his sack'" (Gen. 44:1).

Visualize the Hebrew caravan, lighthearted and in a festive mood, eager to share all with Jacob, as they retraced their steps homeward. Then suddenly, as would happen to their descendants centuries later, Egyptian chariots interrupted their "exodus." The Egyptians leveled charges of disloyalty, dishonesty, and thievery. How could the Hebrews, given the generosity of the prime minister, have returned evil for good? How could they dare steal his silver divining cup after he had treated them so well?

The previous incident of money in the sack should have tempered their self-assured enthusiasm just a bit, but so confident were the brothers that they did not have the cup that they voluntered that if the royal vessel should be among them, the person in whose sack it was found would be put to death and the rest of the brothers would be bondservants to Joseph. However, unbeknown to them, the punishment they suggest doesn't fit Joseph's scenario, and so the steward replies, according to the instruction given him, that "he with whom it is found shall be my servant; and *ye shall be blameless*" (Gen. 44:10, KJV).

The search of the sacks began, starting with the eldest on down toward the youngest. Doubtless Joseph had designed the details of his test long before and had probably instructed the steward to be present also at the banquet to study the faces of the brothers in their exact order around the banquet table. He must commit them to memory so as to be able correctly to progress from Reuben to Benjamin. I can imagine this servant counting brothers instead of sheep the previous night so as to make certain that he has the order right! "Let's see, the one with the touch of gray in his beard, he is the first; then the one whose nose is a bit larger; then the one with the mole on his left cheek," and so on. Joseph had insisted that he open the sacks in precise order! The "judgment" would progress from eldest to youngest. As the Egyptians untied each sack, from Reuben's on downward, the suspense mounted till it must have been suffocating when they reached the sack of the youngest. Sadder words could not be penned: "And the cup was found in Benjamin's sack" (verse 12, KJV).

No words can properly convey the dismay and despair of the brothers now as they trudged back. Before, on the way out from Egypt toward home, their spirits had been high and their steps light. Now, with hearts and clothes ripped apart in anguish, their spirits were low and their feet heavy. As they saw the prime minister's headquarters in the distance, a sense of dread and foreboding overwhelmed them.

"And Judah and his brethren came to Joseph's house; for *he was yet there*" (verse 14, KJV). Although the brothers had begun their homeward expedition, Joseph hadn't gone anywhere. He knew their return was imminent as he awaited their reaction to his test. I imagine him in his royal quarters quietly pondering these latest events and their outcome. Joseph had devised this third and final test so as to place the brothers in a position that once and for all would reveal if their characters had changed. It was Dothan revisited!

Benjamin, Joseph's only full brother, was now under arrest and slated for a sentence of slavery, the *exact prospect* that Joseph had faced 20 years earlier. For a few paltry pieces of silver the brothers had conspired to commit him to a life of Egyptian bondage, knowing full well that his absence and presumed death would pierce their father's heart like an awl. Twenty years earlier, with calculated coldness, the brothers had ignored their consciences as they resorted to falsehood and deception about Joseph's whereabouts, dipping his special coat in goat's blood and exhibiting it before Jacob with mock uncertainty. "We came across this; we're not sure if it's his. Maybe you can recognize it." Without question they had known that such news would crush their father, but they hadn't cared.

Now at last the stage had been set, and the players had taken their positions. Joseph had written the script, but the complete story line had yet to be acted out. This time the brothers could tell the *truth* and still send the son of Rachel to slavery. Then they could return home, according to the express word of the arresting officer, *"blameless."* For once they didn't have to lie to Dad. They didn't have to manipulate the facts. And this time no goat had to die to cover their wickedness. It would be a hundredfold *easier* this time to let the brother be enslaved in Egypt—easier, that is, except for one thing. But that one thing made all the difference in the world! Because when you come right down to it, the now-transformed brothers *couldn't* send Benjamin to bondage.

Joseph had been hoping that his brothers had developed a sense of compassion during his absence. His encounters with them so far had indicated the possibility that their hearts might have softened, that greed and envy were not the primary motives fueling their thoughts. But this last test! It would be so easy for them to do *nothing* and just let events take their course. "Too bad about Benjamin," they could truthfully tell their father, "but it was out of our hands. There was nothing we could do." How would they respond?

As they returned, one look told Joseph that things really had changed. Twenty years before, when the brothers had sold him at Dothan, their expressions had ranged from smirks to apathy as they handed him over to the Ishmaelites. But the faces of the brothers today told a different story. Joseph saw anguish, concern, heartfelt compassion, and anxiety regarding how to redeem Benjamin from bondage. The brothers displayed extreme dismay and trepidation regarding how this news would affect their father.

At this point it was Judah who stepped to the forefront, the very brother who at Dothan had suggested that they dispose of Joseph to the Ishmaelites. But he was not really the same person as before. No longer was he the Judah who could sell his brother and destroy his father. Something was different about him—and all the older brothers, for that matter. This Judah had been converted. He cared a great deal about his father now. In fact, before they left home to come to Egypt, he had pledged his life in behalf of Benjamin to assure Jacob that his youngest son would return.

Now, in one of the most impassioned and emotional speeches of the Bible, and of all antiquity for that matter, Judah pleaded for Benjamin's life. With eloquence and fervor he begged, "Take me instead." With Christlike compassion Judah offered to be his brother's substitute. "I'll take his place as a slave. I'll serve his sentence. Do whatever you want to me, but there is no way I can go home to my father without him. I would rather do anything else than break his heart and see his sorrow."

With this revelation of transformed character Joseph could no longer hold himself back. He had to tell them who he really was. His voice choking and his eyes flooding with tears, he ordered his servants from the room, for what was about to happen was a moment that only a family could share. "I am Joseph," he declared.

A fireworks of thought exploded in the brothers' minds, creating a shock wave that rocked their very beings. Questions crowded their brains, each demanding to be answered first. "Is this really Joseph?" "How could this be our brother whom we sold?" "How did he go from slave to prime minister?" "What will he do to us now?" "Has he been waiting all this time to get his revenge?" "Will he now pay us back for what we did to him?" "Will we be executed?" So many questions!

At the same time things that had seemed strange and mysterious moments before now appeared as clear as day. Suddenly the enigma of how they had been placed at the banquet table in order from eldest to youngest now made sense. His relentless curiosity about their father and younger brother was now understandable. They could now comprehend why the money had been returned in their sacks both times, and even grasp the mystery of the silver cup in Benjamin's sack.

With Joseph's continuing reassurances of his forgiveness and with his perspective on how God had guided through the events of his life, the brothers could now view the prime minister in a different light. Before he had seemed difficult and harsh, hard to get along with, and impossible to understand. He had accused them and put them into difficult situations. But in the end he had turned out to be a tenderhearted, forgiving, loving brother! Now it was Joseph's supreme desire "that where I am, there ye may be also."

Although played out some 16 centuries or so before Gethsemane, the story of Joseph is also the narrative of Jesus, the brother we all sold. Let's not put all the blame on the "Judah" of the New Testament, because all of us participated in the act of betrayal that Thursday night. Maybe we weren't there in person to collect the coins of betrayal or plant the traitor's kiss, but countless times we've sold Him cheaply, for the currency of fleeting desires and transitory lusts. Yet He is now on the throne, having forgiven all, holding no grudge, awaiting the time when He can be reunited with His own.

Before that day comes, though, God permits us to encounter those circumstances that reveal whether or not we have allowed the converting power of His grace to operate in our lives. Are we the same selfish beings that we once were? Is the carnal nature predominant in our lives? Do the lower passions rule? Is our claim to Christianity supported by the evidence of our lives? As Joseph tested the sons of Israel, so God tests us, hoping that we will make the right choices in our lives. The purpose of the pre-Advent judgment is to determine the sincerity of the profession of those who have claimed to be God's sons and daughters. When it is evident that God's people would rather do anything else than break the heart of the Father by sinning, then He will reveal Himself and come to claim them as His own.

Notice that in this model of the investigative judgment contained in the illustration of Joseph, only the "children of Israel" underwent any testing. We have no reason to believe that others who came to buy grain had their money put back into their sacks, or that they received invitations to eat in the palace and were given disproportionate servings, or that anyone hid the silver cup in their sacks. Only those who professed to be "brothers" had to demonstrate that their characters had changed. Peter says that "judgment [must] begin at the house of God" (1 Peter 4:17). Some of the other narratives we've looked at, such as that of the Flood and the destruction of Sodom and Gomorrah, portray the investigative judgment in the context of an examination of wickedness preparatory to judgment and destruction, as well as to the salvation of the faithful. In the story of Joseph, however, the review operates in an entirely positive sense. It determines whether the subjects are qualified for companionship with the one on the throne.

The Passover and the Investigative Judgment

The story of Israel's departure from Egypt is one of the clearest types of last-day redemption that the Bible provides. Revelation's seven last plagues echo Egypt's 10 plagues. The heavenly Canaan awaits us, just as did the literal Canaan for them.

As with the flood in Noah's day, the last plague of Egypt was to be a salvation/destruction event. Those who persisted in their in-fidelity and defiance would suffer the death of the eldest. At the same time, the last plague would be the trigger that would finally release God's people from bondage. In the same way, Revelation's sixth and seven plagues, which bring life to the righteous but death to the wicked, herald the coming of Christ. What does the Exodus from Egypt teach us about the investigative judgment?

"Then Moses called for all the elders of Israel and said to them, 'Pick out and take lambs for yourselves according to your families, and kill the Passover lamb. And you shall take a bunch of hyssop, and dip it in the blood that is in the basin, and strike the lintel and the two doorposts with the blood that is in the basin. And none of you shall go out of the door of his house until morning. For the Lord will pass through to strike the Egyptians; and *when He sees the blood* on the lintel and on the two doorposts, the Lord will pass over the door and not allow the destroyer to come into your houses to strike you'" (Ex. 12:21-23).

Wasn't God able to read the hearts of the men and women in Egypt and to know who was righteous and who was not? Didn't His omniscience allow Him to recognize who was to be saved and who was to be destroyed? Why then did God command them to put the blood on the doorposts? And why was it necessary for Him to pass over and *look to see if it was there?*

Certainly He knows all, and without question He was aware that fateful night whom He would spare and who would suffer. But to give them an opportunity to demonstrate their faith by their action, *and* to give them confidence that His actions were not arbitrary, He expressed Himself in words they could easily grasp. In what we might argue was an unnecessary step, God would "look to see" if the blood was there or not before the destroying angel struck.

Couldn't He just have said, "I know what I'm doing. You'll just have to take My word for it that My decisions are fair. After all, I'm God and I know everything"? Yes, in one sense He could have. It would have been His right to do it that way. But it is not His style, not His pattern. As we've seen, it is a part of His plan that His de-cisions not only be fair and righteous but also understood and appreciated as fair and righteous by His creatures. He wants us to be comfortable with every decision He makes, with every judgment He executes. And so He took this extra step with the children of Israel. If it would inspire confidence that His justice is just, God was more than willing to do it. It was not for His own edification, for He already knew the condition of every heart, but for the benefit of those who found it easier to read bloodstained doorposts than the secrets of human hearts.

The Passover is another example of God's condescending to come down to our level, of His communicating through concepts and words that we know. He seeks to assure us that whatever He does, He always does it from a position of knowledge. The Lord looks into a situation before He intervenes. *Thus, He always investigates before He takes action.* If that was His method with ancient Israel on its way to the earthly Canaan, would we expect it to be any different for the Israel of today before it enters the heavenly Canaan?

The Fall of Jerusalem and the Investigative Judgment

God called Israel to be a missionary nation, to share the light of His love with the whole world. Unfortunately, the record shows that Israel consistently failed in its role. Instead of dispensing God's grace, they hoarded it and fell into habitual and persistent patterns of evil. Imitating the false worship and the social life of their neighbors, Israel tolerated violence, injustice, and all manner of crime.

Despite repeated warnings from His messengers (and occasional glimmers of rightdoing, as in the reigns of David, Hezekiah, and Josiah), God eventually had to "file for divorce" and put His beloved "bride" away, sending her into captivity. First Assyria plundered the northern kingdom of Israel; then Babylon conquered Judah—measures that God permitted in an effort to discipline and win back His people.

Even though God justifiably allowed these military campaigns, and even though, having put up with centuries of sin, He owed the Israelites no explanation as to these fierce judgments, as we have seen, it is not His approach to administer justice without first expressing His intent to examine the situation "one more time," in human language "making sure" that the punishment is deserved.

Speaking through His prophet Zephaniah, whose ministry took place during the reign of Josiah, He stated: "And it shall come to pass at that time that I will search Jerusalem with lamps, and punish the men who are settled in complacency, who say in their heart, 'The Lord will not do good, nor will He do evil'" (Zeph. 1:12).

God's people had come to the point that they believed that He had little to do with the affairs of their everyday lives. According to them, He didn't know, or He didn't care, what happened. The belief that He was not involved gave them the excuse they were looking for to continue their selfish way of living.

We might ask, Did God really need to light a lamp (or "candle," KJV) and search the streets of Jerusalem like a divine Diogenes to see if there were any honest in heart among the inhabitants? In His omniscience, didn't He already know completely the conditions that existed? Of course He did, just as He fully knew the iniquity of Sodom and the cities of the plain. But to gain the confidence of His subjects, God employed this human way of doing things. He would condescend to communicate in a language that we understand so that we could be comfortable that "He knows" before "He does." *As always, He investigates before He takes action.*

It seems, however, that the sins of Judah were so clear that little searching was necessary. Through Jeremiah, the contemporary of Zephaniah, God said: "On your skirts is found the blood of the lives of the poor innocents. I have not found it by secret search, but plainly on all these things" (Jer. 2:34).

Much of the testimony of the prophets who spoke just before Jerusalem's fall is a sad chronicle of Israel's failure to live up to its light, told from heaven's viewpoint. Once again, as has been His consistent pattern, *He investigated before He took action.*

The Fall of Babylon and the Investigative Judgment

Scripture frequently uses the story of the fall of Babylon to illustrate what will happen just prior to Jesus' return. The book of Revelation is saturated with allusions to Babylon's fall and the lessons it provides. What does the story of the fall of Babylon teach us about the investigative judgment and God's dealings with His creatures?

Nebuchadnezzar made three attacks against Jerusalem, and by the time the city fell in 586 B.C., the king of Babylon had raided the Temple and thoroughly confiscated its treasures to adorn his own temple museum, a demonstration in his view that his gods were superior to the God of the Israelites. His victory indicated that Nebo, Marduk, and their fellow deities were more powerful than Jehovah. Military conflict back then wasn't just "my soldiers against your soldiers"—it was also "my gods against your gods."

A story that uniquely models Israel's failures to share the knowledge of God with her neighbors took place more than a century earlier. When God promised to heal Hezekiah, He sent a sign, turning back the shadow on the sundial 10 degrees, an event that obviously affected not only those in Jerusalem but elsewhere. The account in Isaiah 38 and 39 does not explicitly tell us that the envoys from Babylon came to investigate the phenomenon of the mysterious sundial, but given their interest in the movements of the planets and stars, it seems highly likely that they would have inquired as to the cause of the strange event. If so, they would have foreshadowed the arrival of the Magi centuries later, when they came to Jerusalem in search of answers. But when the Babylonian ambassadors reached Jerusalem, Hezekiah proudly showed them all his treasures, both in the palace and the Temple.

After they had gone, Hezekiah received a visit from Isaiah. The prophet asked to what use the king had put his opportunity to share knowledge of the Creator-God, who not only could heal disease but also controlled the entire universe. Sadly, Hezekiah was forced to admit that he had shared with them only things, not theology—"goods," but not God. Isaiah then predicted that someday the people from the East would return, relieve Jerusalem of its treasures, and also take its sons and daughters into captivity.

That day came when the armies of Nebuchadnezzar conquered Jerusalem, removing the sacred Temple vessels and ornaments (see Jer. 52:17-20). The objects rested in Babylon's royal museum for decades. Meanwhile, Nebuchadnezzar, through the influence of Daniel and his friends, found the Lord and became a true follower of God. But later his grandson Belshazzar ascended to the throne. He was technically coregent with his father, Nabonidus, but because of some recent squabbles with the powerful priests of Babylon, the latter had decided to escape the political heat and take up residence at his palace in Tema, in Arabia, leaving his son in charge in Babylon.

Being familiar with the royal family, no doubt Daniel had had many an opportunity to hold Belshazzar on his knee as a toddler. Without question the young prince had heard the valuable lessons learned by his grandfather Nebuchadnezzar. In addition, he must have known of the great statue dream, with its prediction of another kingdom replacing Babylon in world influence.

It's also possible that Belshazzar might have learned the message of Daniel's visions, that the bear would come after the lion. And somewhere along the line the Hebrew prophet might have mentioned the prophecy of Isaiah that predicted that Cyrus the Persian would conquer Babylon. But Belshazzar chose not to follow his grandfather in service to Jehovah. Instead, he steeled his heart in rebellion.

Then came the news of the advancing Medo-Persian troops under the generalship of Cyrus. City after city fell to Cyrus's military machine. It conquered the nearby city of Opis, and Sippar, 35 miles north of Babylon, succumbed to Cyrus just two days before the events described in Daniel 5.

How would Belshazzar respond to the threat? Would he double the guard and put everyone on 24-hour alert? The continuing victories of Cyrus's armies confirmed the prophecy. But Belshazzar closed his eyes to the evidence. After all, wasn't Babylon the eternal city? Weren't its walls impregnable? Wasn't its water and food supply able to withstand any siege? Hadn't its gods protected it in the past? Why should Belshazzar worry about some dusty predictions of foreign soothsayers? Who cared what Jehovah said? Wasn't His city of Jerusalem in ruins now, His Temple demolished? Weren't the vessels that once adorned that Temple right now in Babylon, in Belshazzar's temple museum?

At this perilous time in Babylon's history, in a defiance that approached insanity, Belshazzar scheduled a party for his lords and instructed that his stewards go to the temple museum and retrieve those vessels that had come from Jerusalem's Temple and use them as the goblets and glasses at his banquet. "We will see what becomes of the predictions of Jehovah," Belshazzar implied through his response. "We will see if a chest of silver replaces the head of gold. I will defy His prophets and their predictions by using the very articles that came from the house of their God."

Archaeologists may have identified the very room where this riotous display took place. Babylon's Southern Palace, which was essentially the residence of Belshazzar, had a throne room measuring 173 feet long, 57 feet wide, and 66 feet high. It was the only room large enough to accommodate the number of guests that the Bible describes the king as entertaining that night.

As Belshazzar's bash began, the drinking and laughter commenced. Toasts and jokes, music and mirth, arose, filling the air with boisterous commotion. "They drank wine, and praised the gods of gold and silver, bronze and iron, wood and stone" (Dan. 5:4). I wonder if anyone remembered the statue of "gold and silver, bronze and iron"? As the evening continued eyes became glazed and voices hoarse as king and guests tried to outdo one another in disorderly conduct.

Suddenly a shocked silence spread across the room. Heads turned to find out what had interrupted their revelry. Eyes widened and faces blanched as on the plaster wall "over against the candlestick" (Dan. 5:5, KJV) letters of fire appeared, inscribing a cryptic message written by a mysterious hand.

Desperately Belshazzar sought an explanation for what was happening, summoning the wise men, the astrologers, the soothsayers—anyone who could interpret the enigmatic message. But despite offers of riches and honor to anyone who could decipher the writing, all the wise men of Babylon failed, just as they did decades before when questioned about Nebuchadnezzar's dream.

Frantically Belshazzar attempted to find some way to solve the mystery without having to resort to the aged Hebrew prophet, but found none. After all other avenues were exhausted, the queen mother came to the banquet hall and suggested that they consult Daniel, who had "the Spirit of the Holy God" (Dan. 5:11). Embarrassed and humiliated before his guests, Belshazzar had no other alternative but to summon the Hebrew prophet.

It is interesting to note that one of the inducements Belshazzar offered to anyone who might interpret the inscription was the position of being "third ruler in the kingdom" (verse 7). Because of what we now know regarding the coregency of Belshazzar and his father, Nabonidus (whom up until about a hundred years ago, scholars listed as the last king of Babylon, with no mention of Belshazzar whatsoever), it was the highest reward the king could offer!

When the aged prophet, now in his 80s, arrived, his eyes quickly took in the scene, including the handwriting on the wall and the blasphemous use of the sacred Temple objects. Belshazzar demanded, "Are you that Daniel who is one of the captives from Judah . . . ? *I have heard of you*" (verses 13, 14). No doubt it was one of the greatest understatements of history! Be assured, Belshazzar had more than "heard of" the prophet. The self-willed king had made a career of beating back the quiet impulses and gentle nudging of the Holy Spirit. For years he had been repressing those lessons, those memories, that could have brought salvation and light.

Before interpreting the message of the flaming letters, Daniel contrasted how Nebuchadnezzar, his grandfather, had accepted God with how Belshazzar had resisted. In words that must have cut Belshazzar to the heart, Daniel said, "But you his [grandson], Belshazzar, have not humbled your heart, although *you knew all this*" (verse 22).

God is not unfair in His judgments against His creatures. He does not hold us accountable for that which we do not know or could not have known. In addition, He recognizes all the circumstances and variables in each situation. "The Lord shall count, when He writeth [the Hebrew word is *kathab,* the same word translated "written" in Daniel 12:1] up the people, that this man was born there" (Ps. 87:6, KJV). "To him who knows to do good and does not do it, to him it is sin" (James 4:17).

The standard to which God held Belshazzar was a fair one, based on his own experience and opportunities, and Daniel reminded him that he was not ignorant of the divine principles. The prophet pointed out the blasphemy in Belshazzar's usage of the sacred Temple articles in his defiant feast.

Then Daniel turned his attention to the writing on the wall and quickly discerned the play on words used to convey the message of doom. *Mene, mene* (from the Hebrew *manah,* meaning "to count"): the word occurs twice to emphasize the scrutiny and carefulness of the examination. In other words, "God has gone over your records and checked them twice."

Tekel means "to be weighed." People in ancient times used scales to weigh metals as a test of their value, and as a result, they became a symbol to represent judicial examination. The Egyptian Book of the Dead pictured a person's heart placed on one side of the scales, a feather on the other, to determine the individual's merit to enter the afterlife. The symbol of scales still represents fairness in the courtroom, as witnessed in the sculpture *Blind Justice.* In other words, God was saying to the king of Babylon, "Your case has been placed in the divine scales of justice," and under divine inspiration the prophet adds, "and found wanting."

Upharsin comes from the Aramaic *peras* (Hebrew *paras*), meaning "to divide," "part," "deal," "tear," "halve hooves." (It is used most often to describe the dividing of hooves, which, along with the chewing of the cud, qualified an animal as being clean.) God could have employed many words to describe the disintegration of the Babylonian kingdom, but He chose one that could uniquely encompass the "act" as well as the "actor," since *peres* is the root for the word "Persia," the kingdom that would conquer Babylon before the next sunrise. Daniel used this form of the word in his explanation. It is a play on words to predict the event (the "dividing," or "breaking") by the agent (the Persians).

God gave His indictment from an accounting point of view: "Your records have been called in for a divine audit. They have been double-checked, and your account is short." It represents a metallurgical point of view: "You have been assayed in the divine scales and shown to be unworthy."

As in Jeremiah's indictment of Jerusalem, the bellows of purification had blown, the refining process had taken place, but the divine Smelter had labored in vain, and wickedness still remained. Now God had declared Babylon to be discarded metal, for the Lord had rejected it (see Jer. 6:27-30; Mal. 3:3).

Even as Daniel was speaking, and the royal tailor was fitting him with the robe of honor in a kingdom whose existence was now measured in minutes, Cyrus's armies were about to enter the city. More than a century earlier, the prophet Isaiah had foretold: "Thus says the Lord to His anointed, to Cyrus, whose right hand I have held—to subdue nations before him and loose the armor of kings, to open before him the double doors, so that the gates will not be shut" (Isa. 45:1). And now, in an exact fulfillment of the prophecy, Babylon's gates were left open, and the invading forces entered the capital with virtually no resistance. Babylon fell, Belshazzar was slain, and God's word came true.

Twenty-five centuries later, as we sift through the story, it gives us an accurate picture of divine justice at work. God had provided numerous opportunities for Belshazzar to accept Him. He had made His mercy abundant. But because of relentless obstinacy and unchecked rebellion, the king and his kingdom had finally passed the point of no return. They had placed themselves outside the boundaries of divine forbearance, and now God had to act.

But before the gavel of divine justice fell, God stooped to give the rebellious king a message, indicating that the verdict was a just one, that He had reviewed Belshazzar's case with divine scrutiny. As with Sodom and Gomorrah, God had inquired and looked into the matter, conducting a celestial inquest before executing the sentence. Once again we ask: Did God's omniscience not work concerning Babylon? Was God not fully aware of its sins? Was He blind to its arrogance and pride? Was the Divine Watcher not paying attention to the attitudes and conduct of the Babylonian kingdom? Obviously God was fully aware of Babylon's legacy of wickedness.

But in condescension He lowered Himself to speak in a language we could easily understand. To vindicate the terrible verdict He was about to pronounce, He employed vocabulary that we are familiar with. He had looked into the record book and had satisfied Himself that the cup of iniquity was full. As pertains to our study, the emphatic repetition of the word mene as part of the writing on the wall is instructive—it underscores that God goes the second mile in the direction of fairness. It says: "Your account has been double-checked."

As we have seen now on many occasions, He *investigated before He took action.* If He conducted Himself in that way with respect to literal Babylon, would we not also expect a "numbering," an "accounting," a "weighing," a divine inquiry, with respect to apocalyptic Babylon?

The Woman Taken in Adultery
and the Investigative Judgment

I realize that some ancient biblical manuscripts do not contain the story of the woman taken in adultery, but it seems so consistent with our Lord's character, as well as with that of those who opposed His ministry, that it clearly belongs in the scriptural canon. (Although many today regard the woman in the story as Mary Magdalene, the Bible nowhere makes that specific identification.)

Desperate to find a way to trap Jesus and stop His growing popularity, the scribes and Pharisees devised a plan that they were certain would place Him squarely on the horns of an inescapable dilemma, and He would find Himself in an untenable position. "Then the scribes and Pharisees brought to Him a woman caught in adultery. And when they had set her in the midst, they said to Him, 'Teacher, this woman was caught in adultery, in the very act. Now Moses, in the law, commanded us that such should be stoned. But what do You say'" (John 8:3-5).

The Jews thought they had Jesus cornered, because if He answered that they should stone the woman, then He would be violating Roman occupation law, since only the representative of

Caesar could issue a death decree. On the other hand, if He directed her release, He would be going against the law of Moses, and they would have something to accuse Him of.

Interestingly, the narrative makes no mention of the male participant in the adultery! Apparently a double standard provided him an escape hatch from the embarrassing position into which the religious leaders had thrust the woman. It doesn't take much reading between the lines to discern a conspiracy, a setup, in which no doubt the man involved was a participant.

At first Jesus seemed to ignore them, then stooped to scribble something on what must have been a dusty Temple pavement. It seems that this story took place the day after the conclusion of the "feast" (John 7:37), referring to the Feast of Tabernacles (John 7:2), an autumn convocation of which the Day of Atonement was a significant part. This festival, according to the historian Josephus, frequently attracted to Jerusalem more than a million people from all over the world, who constructed temporary dwellings of palm fronds or other material to commemorate Israel's wilderness-wandering experience. Even the people who lived in Jerusalem would typically erect a tent or tree branch tabernacle on their rooftop to participate in the festival.

The Temple would have been an especially crowded place, with multitudes jostling and elbowing within its halls and porches. Since the feast had ended the day before, people would have been dismantling their shelters and readying themselves for their return trip home. In all the commotion the pavements would not have been in their cleanest state, allowing a ready surface for Christ to use as a slate.

Again the scribes and Pharisees verbally prodded Him, demanding an answer to their question. This time Jesus asserted: "He who is without sin among you, let him throw a stone at her first" (John 8:7). Once more He scribbled on the Temple pavement.

What might Christ have been writing? Many Bible students believe that it was the sins of the accusers, perhaps so cryptically that no one but the wrongdoer would understand it, but nevertheless clear enough so that each accuser there knew that Jesus was aware that every one of them was hiding something.

Let's test that possibility. Did Christ have the capability of knowing human hearts and deeds? Yes, He did—both the good and the bad. When He met Nathanael, who wondered whether any good thing could come from Nazareth, Jesus said to him, "Before Philip called you, when you were under the fig tree, I saw you" (John 1:48). Jesus said to the woman at the well: "'Go, call your husband, and come here.' The woman answered and said, 'I have no husband.' Jesus said to her, 'You have well said, "I have no husband," for you have had five husbands, and the one whom you now have is not your husband; in that you spoke truly'" (John 4:16-18).

One time the friends of a paralytic, frustrated by the crowds surrounding Jesus at a certain house, dismantled the roof and lowered the invalid, on his pallet, in front of the Savior, who had compassion on him and said, "Man, your sins are forgiven you" (Luke 5:20), a statement that must have encouraged him, since the Jews of Jesus' day looked upon personal suffering as divine judgment.

Instantly the scribes and Pharisees choked over the possibility that Christ had the authority to forgive sins. They correctly understood that it was a prerogative belonging only to God, and would constitute blasphemy were a mere mortal to claim it. However, they were wrong in their refusal to accept Jesus as being more than a mere man, when He was indeed the incarnate God. "But when Jesus *perceived their thoughts,* He answered and said to them, 'Why are you reasoning in your hearts?'" (Luke 5:22).

One Sabbath in the synagogue Jesus healed a man with a withered hand. The scribes and Pharisees had been watching Him closely to see if they could manufacture some accusation against Him. "But He knew their thoughts" (Luke 6:8). John states plainly: "He knew all men, and had no need that anyone should testify of man, for He knew what was in man" (John 2:24, 25).

Yes, Christ certainly had the capability to know that the heart of each of the troublemakers who had brought him the adulterous woman was not "sincere," but "sin-seared." Whatever it was that He wrote in the dust, it certainly had the effect of making the accusers uncomfortable, because they began to withdraw from the scene, eventually leaving the woman alone with Jesus. John 8:9 says that they were "convicted by their conscience," an understandable reaction if He had just written their sins in the dust.

Let's assume for the sake of argument that what Jesus inscribed in the dust was the record of the transgressions of those pharisaical accusers, something certainly within His capability. It was also consistent with His character not to expose sinners openly for what they were, yet to convey the message to the sinner that their secrets were known to Him, as illustrated in the exchange with Judas at the Last Supper.

If this indeed was the case, then it presents a compelling *acted* parable of the judgment. As we can turn a jewel one way and then another, allowing the light to reflect on its various facets, so the Bible sometimes presents topics of interest and importance from different perspectives. This model presents the judgment from a different view, demonstrating that in one sense Christ's enemies initiated the judgment. The Pharisees demanded the inquisition and summoned the woman before Christ for condemnation, hoping in the process to hinder His work and tarnish His character and reputation. It was their whole purpose for the charade. They occupied the role of the "accuser of the brethren," bringing charges against God's children, intending in the process to defame Christ's character.

We should emphasize that, while we have been viewing the judgment as it applies to humanity, its function from a wider perspective is to clear God's name of the accusations brought by the devil. In this episode we've seen that the skirmish was between the Pharisees and Christ. The woman was merely the tool they used to attack Him. (Keep in mind that a "woman" many times in the Bible represents the church). As the drama unfolded, Jesus pronounced her acquittal, but the encounter was not really about her—it was about the Jewish leaders' attempt to destroy Christ. In a similar way, the judgment isn't by any means just about removing the condemnation of the righteous—it's primarily about vindicating God's name. Christ's death on the cross wasn't just about saving humanity, although that certainly was a vital aspect.

His victory over sin removed the tarnish placed on God's name and character by the enemy. After all is said and done, with a great crescendo the song will rise: "Great and marvelous are Your works, Lord God Almighty! Just and true are Your ways, O King of the saints!" (Rev. 15:3).

The image of Christ silently writing the sins of the accusers in the sand gives us a clear picture of God's character. Even Jesus' posture is relevant: He "stooped." His condescension to deal with the disease of sin began in heaven, continued on this earth, and will forever be a part of His character. Humility is the hallmark of divinity.

At the heart of God's character is agape love, which is reluctant to parade the sins of others, a character trait His children could well emulate. Although He knows all, He is loath to expose human misdeeds. He is a living expression of that love that does not "gloat over other men's sins" (1 Cor. 13:6, NEB). Jesus was 1 Corinthians 13 in sandals. We have no record that Christ announced publicly the sins of the woman at the well. Even his betrayer He treated with respect and kindness, so that at the Last Supper, after He had shared with Judas the morsel (actually a Middle Eastern symbol of affection), the rest of the disciples had no idea what had happened. As Judas left the upper room they thought he was going out for some more food or perhaps to make a contribution for the poor (John 13:29).

Reluctant to expose our sins, God is more than willing to forgive and forget them, to bury them in the depths of the sea and blot them out of His record book, but since He prizes the individual's freedom of choice so highly, He does not force or coerce the conscience. Thus, if a person persistently clings to sin and exhibits the symptoms of that failed relationship with God through wrong behavior, the Lord is aware of what is happening even though the individual thinks that he or she has done the sins in secret. The record of the wrongs remains.

When men and women at last face the heavenly account of their wickedness, shame and guilt will drive them from the presence of their Maker, a reaction whose roots penetrate back to the very soil of Eden. That is what Adam and Eve did when they first sinned, and so it will be at the end. Voluntarily he or she will withdraw from the company of the one whose holiness and righteousness they at that moment find extremely discomforting. We see this reality reflected in the exodus of the accusers in John 8. At the end the wicked, because they didn't run to the Rock, will run to the rocks. And because they didn't hide themselves in the cleft of the Rock, as did Moses, they will try to conceal themselves in the clefts of the rocks when He returns. The judgment is not about God's arbitrarily saying who's going to be saved or lost, but about people's disqualifying themselves of their own volition. All the lost will face the record of their spurned opportunities to accept God's provision for salvation.

We see also from John 8 that there will come a time when human words will cease. The accusations, indictments, and excuses that human beings have been industriously devising since humanity's fall will finally end. In the story of the woman caught in adultery, the accusers, once incessantly demanding that Christ answer their questions, became strangely silent. Now they had nothing more to say. As in the parable of the man confronted by his rejection of the wedding garment, they were speechless (see Matt. 22:12) and wanted only to escape as quickly as possible.

An interesting parallel is that they left in the same sequence as prevailed in the seating at Joseph's banquet table and the searching of the sacks for the silver cup. "Then those who heard it, being convicted by their conscience, went out one by one, *beginning with the oldest even to the last*" (John 8:9). This is consistent with other scriptures describing the progression of the judgment: "They began with the elders who were before the temple" (Eze. 9:6).

Thus the story of the woman taken in adultery tells us much about God's judgment and His dealings with sinners.

The Second Fall of Jerusalem
and the Investigative Judgment

Following its return from the Babylonian captivity, Judah received the opportunity to rebuild. True to the prophetic Word, Jerusalem prospered under the ministries of Ezra, Nehemiah,

Haggai, Zerubbabel, and others. The Persian Empire allowed, even encouraged, Jews to return to their homeland and make a new beginning! The nation could have had a glorious future had Jerusalem truly consecrated itself to following God's will. Unfortunately, the sacred record tells us that by Malachi's time, like stubborn diehard crabgrass, many of the same sins that had brought about Jerusalem's fall had sprouted and again flourished.

About 400 years after the preaching of Malachi the angels proclaimed the birth of the Christ child. The first coming of Christ to earth had many missions to accomplish, but we will consider one specific perspective: before Jerusalem would again be destroyed, before the last part of Daniel 9 would be fulfilled and the people of the Roman prince would receive divine permission to conduct siege warfare against the city, God Himself in the person of Jesus Christ would "come down to see" and experience firsthand its rebellion against His will, its obstinate refusal to comply with heaven's plan.

History confirms that Jerusalem didn't accept Him, killing Him instead. Like the literal children of Israel, who didn't recognize Joseph in his glory, these children of Israel knew not Jesus in His humility. Instead of honoring Him as the Lord, they executed Him as an imposter. Only days before this traumatic event, Jesus said: "Hear another parable: There was a certain landowner who planted a vineyard and set a hedge around it, dug a winepress in it and built a tower. And he leased it to vinedressers and went into a far country. Now when vintage-time drew near, he sent his servants to the vinedressers, that they might receive its fruit. And the vinedressers took his servants, beat one, killed one, and stoned another. Again he sent other servants, more than the first, and they did likewise to them. Then last of all he sent his son to them, saying 'They will respect my son.' But when the vinedressers saw the son, they said among themselves, 'This is the heir. Come, let us kill him and seize his inheritance.' So they took him and cast him out of the vineyard and killed him" (Matt. 21:33-39).

Through the centuries God had sent His prophetic messengers to do an accounting and obtain the fruitage, but His people had grossly mistreated them. Now, "last of all," He sent His Son. And as the parable predicted, they murdered Him and thus sealed their destiny.

Following His triumphant entry into Jerusalem the Sunday before His death, Jesus encountered a fig tree. "The next day, when they had come out from Bethany, He was hungry. And seeing from afar a fig tree having leaves, He went to see if perhaps He would find something on it. When He came to it, He found nothing but leaves, for it was not the season for figs. In response Jesus said to it, 'Let no one eat fruit from you ever again'" (Mark 11:12-14).

Did Jesus have something personal against the fig tree? That would seem out of character. No, we might consider it an acted parable, reflecting His mission to the Jewish nation, symbolized aptly by the fig tree. Like this tree, Israel was luxuriantly garbed in the appearance of faith, but further inspection showed its leadership to be devoid of the genuine fruit of heart religion. As pertains to our study, notice carefully the expression *"He went to see* if perhaps He would find something on it" that precedes the pronouncement of judgment against it. *There was investigation before action.*

Notice also the usage of the third-person imperative in the phrase "Let no one eat fruit from you ever again." It is clear that the Jewish leadership rejected their role as heralds of the Messiah, and that God would not coerce them to change, but would sadly allow them to remain in their rebellious condition. The "curse" expressed was not so much a divine imprecation as it was God's acknowledgment of the (wrong) decision that they had forged despite knowing the drastic consequences it would bring. This real-life dramatization of the "coming down to see" inquiry into the character of His people foreshadows the investigative judgment to take place before the end. If divine justice operated this way at Christ's first advent, would it not be reasonable to expect that it would follow a similar pattern at His second advent?

Remembering Nebuchadnezzar's past destruction of Jerusalem and realizing that the Romans would attack the city in the future, Jesus might have said, "Jerusalem is fallen, is fallen." Because He knew that in only a few days its inhabitants would seal their doom by crucifying Him, He felt Himself overcome with grief. With tears in His voice He put the "handwriting on the wall." Jerusalem had been weighed and found wanting. Its reign as "a kingdom of priests and a holy nation" (Ex. 19:6) was numbered and finished. Another entity, the Christian church, would now fulfill the role of sharing the truth about God with the world: "O Jerusalem, Jerusalem, the one who kills the prophets and stones those who are sent to her! How often I wanted to gather your children together, as a hen gathers her chicks under her wings, but you were not willing! See! Your house is left to you desolate'" (Matt. 23:37, 38).

The word "desolate" in Christ's pronouncement is pregnant with meaning. This "house," or Temple, was not the one built by Solomon and blessed by the visible presence of God (1 Kings 8:10, 11). Nebuchadnezzar had destroyed that Temple in 586 B.C. Since then it had been rebuilt under Zerubbabel and then Herod.

But the promise had been given that the glory of the rebuilt Temple would exceed that of Solomon's (Haggai 2:3-9), a promise fulfilled by the visible, tangible ministry of Jesus, the incarnate God, whose presence honored its confines. In His human life Christ was there at His dedication and then when He was 12, just beginning to catch a glimpse of His "Father's business." During the days of His ministry He frequently visited it. How often His gracious words rang from her walls and porches as He shared the truth of His Father's kingdom! How often spontaneous exclamations of joy resulting from His miracles of healing echoed through her arches! Yes, the glory of Solomon's Temple was impressive, with its architectural beauty and inaugurating Shekinah cloud (1 Kings 8:10, 11). But the glory of Herod's rebuilt Temple had indeed surpassed it, for its real majesty was the glory of God as revealed to Moses. It was the daily personal revelation of the character of God, who is "merciful and gracious, longsuffering, and abounding in goodness and truth" (Ex. 34:6).

Because of their rejection of Him, the Temple would no longer be privileged to have Him as its occupant, and without Him that building, or any structure of worship, for that matter, would be empty and desolate.

After Calvary, for 40 more years the building would see countless sacrificial offerings whose significance had been overshadowed by the death of the Lamb of God. Then would come the armies of Titus the Roman, who would lay its foundations bare, leaving it "desolate," a word lifted directly from the pages of Daniel's prophecy (Dan. 9:27). Titus would accomplish in the physical realm what had already existed as a spiritual reality for four decades.

With the protection of divine grace being withdrawn, she was going to be handed over to the "breakers," in a destruction so complete that "not one stone shall be left here upon another" (Matt. 24:2). Daniel's "abomination of desolation" (Dan. 9:27), explained by Jesus as being "Jerusalem surrounded by armies" (Luke 21:20), would arrive under the leadership of Titus. But, as His pattern is, before the terrible judgment would fall, before His city would be demolished, God would pay a personal visit to it.

Yes, Jesus had many reasons for coming to this earth, but don't overlook this one: before Jerusalem's destruction He would personally "come down and see"—*He would investigate before taking action.*

Narrative Study Summary

Having reviewed these narratives, we conclude that they are very clear in their depiction of who God is and how He relates to His creatures; that He has a pattern of *investigating before He takes action* (not because He is uninformed, but to develop in us confidence that He implements His decisions from a position of knowledge). So clear is this revelation of God in the stories throughout the Scriptures that we can boldly state that even if there were no Daniel 8:14, Daniel 12:1, Revelation 14:7, or Revelation 22:12, we would nevertheless anticipate that there would be an investigative judgment prior to Jesus' return.

The various stories teach us that before taking action, God reviews the evidence, whether it involves an individual (Adam, Eve, and Cain), a city (Sodom and Gomorrah), or a kingdom (Judah and Babylon). As far as events of major importance in the scriptural record are concerned, consider the following impressive list, each of which illustrates the pattern of God's investigating before He takes action:

- ❖ the first sin
- ❖ the first murder
- ❖ the first worldwide destruction
- ❖ the Tower of Babel
- ❖ the destruction of Sodom and Gomorrah
- ❖ the Exodus
- ❖ the first destruction of Jerusalem
- ❖ the judgment of Babylon
- ❖ the second destruction of Jerusalem

One would have a hard time finding an example in the biblical record in which God executed judgment in a significant way before first taking that extra step of investigating.

A common theme runs through these narratives—it is of a loving God who desires so strongly that His creatures understand and appreciate the way that He administrates the universe that He is willing to go beyond what is necessary. He is the "God of the second mile." When the Lord lived on earth, the hated Romans occupied Palestine. Their soldiers, barracks, proconsuls, taxes, and laws were an unwelcome but constant reminder of Judah's loss of freedom. Under accepted statutes of the occupation, if a Roman soldier conscripted you to bear his belongings, no matter what you were doing at that time or how busy you were, you were obliged to shoulder them for a distance of up to one mile. From the top of a local hillside Jesus pronounced the radical notion that "whoever compels you to go one mile, go with him two" (Matt. 5:41). His teaching was: Do what is more than the minimal constraint. Go beyond what merely satisfies the requirement.

Jesus never asks us to do something He hasn't already done or to go somewhere He hasn't already been. When He gave that command, and all others from His grassy pulpit, He was saying, "Be like Me." The God of the second mile, He's always done more than just what's necessary. Consider these parallels that illustrate His willingness to do more than the minimal requirement:

1. From Carmel's pinnacle Elijah prayed a short and simple but effective prayer for God to hear him after the priests of Baal had spent most of the day trying to get the attention of their god. God answered with a fire that not only consumed the sacrifice but also the wood, the stones of the altar, the dust, and the water that the prophet had ordered poured over the altar. God went the second mile in responding to Elijah's prayer!

2. Possibly the worst news that anyone could receive in the ancient world came upon Naaman. The Syrian army commander had contracted leprosy, the dreaded disease that caused the skin and appendages to decay and putrify. The military leader was waging a battle he couldn't win. It was a living death with no known cure. At the suggestion of his Israelite servant girl, he went to Elisha for healing. The prophet told him to wash in the Jordan River seven times. With much reluctance, Naaman followed the prophetic prescription, and after the seventh dip God immediately healed him, and "his flesh was restored like the flesh of a little child" (2 Kings 5:14). Naaman would have been thrilled to have the adult skin that he had had before he came down with the disease, to be able to interact with society as he had done before. But instead, God gave him the skin of a child—better than any plastic surgery or mud spa treatment. Try to visualize the revitalized Naaman when he returned home to his family. In grateful amazement they touched and caressed his new skin, soft as a baby's. When he had left, his face was too ugly to look at. But now, what a difference! God went the second mile when He healed Naaman!

3. One day John the Baptist encountered the one whom he recognized as being the Christ, the Messiah, the one who was the focus of his ministry. Jesus asked John to baptize Him. John hesitated, realizing his unworthiness. "But Jesus answered and said to him, 'Permit it to be so now, for thus it is fitting for us to fulfill all righteousness'" (Matt. 3:15).

The symbolic meaning of baptism included confession, repentance, and remission of sin (Matt. 3:6; Acts 2:38). Yet Jesus, the perfect Son of God, had no sin to confess. He was not in need of repentance or forgiveness. Nevertheless, as our Example, He humbly bowed beneath the waters of Jordan. Jesus went the second mile by being baptized.

4. Jesus and His disciples received an invitation to a wedding in Cana. When the beverage supply ran short, Mary informed her Son, who instructed the servants to fill some empty stone pots with water. When they had done so, and then drew from them, they found that it was no longer water, but a most delicious refreshment. When he had tasted it, the host said to the bridegroom, "Every man at the beginning sets out the good wine, and when the guests have well drunk, then the inferior. You have kept the good wine until now!" (John 2:10).

They would have been happy if the quality of second batch had been the same. Nor would they have complained had it been inferior, because that was what everyone expected. But Jesus gave them something better. He went the second mile at Cana!

5. One day Jesus' disciples asked Him whether He had paid the Temple tax. Jesus questioned Peter whether it was customary for aliens to pay this subsidy, and the disciple responded that nonresidents were required to pay the tax. The Lord then stated, "Then the sons are free. Nevertheless, lest we offend them, go to the sea, cast in a hook, and take the fish that comes up first" (Matt. 17:26, 27).

In the mouth of that fish they found a coin sufficient to pay the tax. Think for a moment how utterly ridiculous it was to receive a tax from Jesus for the Temple! He was the High Priest, the Light, the Lamb, the Bread, and the Incense. It would be more preposterous than to charge Beethoven to hear a rendition of his *Fifth Symphony!* But Jesus operated on the "second mile" principle. He was willing to take the extra step if appropriate.

6. In one sense the purpose of Christ's mission in coming to earth was to demonstrate that Adam needn't have transgressed in the garden. It would already have been an incomprehensible condescension for Jesus, the "last Adam," just to have laid aside His glory, His creative powers, and come to our planet in the same condition, stature, and constitution as Adam in order to resist temptation and defeat the devil. But Jesus arrived as a baby, not as an

adult. He lacked the advantage of having a body fresh from the Creator's hand. Instead He tabernacled in a body encumbered with the physical effects of thousands of years of sin and degeneration. It wasn't the Garden of Eden He went to, but a dark and dreary world with all the thorns and thistles, both real and metaphorical, that the centuries had cultivated. Jesus could have chosen to come to the Eden of old and prove the devil wrong, but instead He went the second mile and was born in a stable in Bethlehem!

7. Eighteen centuries before Calvary, Abraham and Isaac had prefigured the event on Mount Moriah, the "mount of God's provision," which later became the location of the Temple in Jerusalem. Tender embraces and tears of compassion preceded the raising of Abraham's arm, bearing its instrument of death. At the last second God halted that arm and directed Abraham to a substitute, a sacrificial animal that took Isaac's place on the altar. In contrast, when Jesus walked that lonely hill, bearing the wood for the sacrifice, he carried the effects of the cruel Roman scourge. "They cut deep wounds in my back and made it like a plowed field" (Ps. 129:3, TEV). He had beatings, not embraces; spitting and mocking insults, not tears of compassion. There could be no visible tokens of the Father's paternal love toward His Son apparent that Friday at Calvary. Yet Jesus willingly gave His life, dying "even the death of the cross" (Phil. 2:8). Dare we reverently suggest that Jesus went "beyond Moriah" to "Golgotha," with all of its repulsive ugliness, accomplishing a "second mile" salvation. No wonder the Bible speaks of "so great salvation," an "abundant entrance" into the kingdom!

With all of these illustrations of God's willingness to go the second mile, should we be amazed, then, that He is prepared to take an extra step in the truly significant matter of forever fixing the fate of His creatures for eternal life or eternal death, so that all are fully convinced of the absolute justice employed in that process? I think not. The Scriptures have repeatedly revealed that He is willing to come down to the level of His sons and daughters and speak their language. Though He is omniscient, He is willing to review the evidence "once more," to inspire His creatures with the confidence that His decisions are based on knowledge and fairness.

Chapter Six

Studying Daniel 8:14 as an Answer to a Specific Question

My wife teaches history in a local community college, and she tells me that once in a while on a test students will write an apparently brilliant answer to a question. Unfortunately, it is obvious that they have misunderstood a key term of the question, and their answer has no relevance to what is being asked. It pays to make sure you have the question right when answering an exam! In a similar vein, it would be well at some point in our study of Daniel 8:14 to pause and realize that the verse actually answers a question posed in verse 13, and that it would be worthwhile for us to consider the meaning and message of that question as we ponder the answer in the next verse: "Then I heard a holy one speaking; and another holy one said to that certain one who was speaking, 'How long will the vision be, concerning the daily sacrifices and the transgression of desolation, the giving of both the sanctuary and the host to be trampled underfoot?'"

What exactly does the question of verse 13 have in mind? We could rephrase the question as: "How long will it be till the end of the trampling, persecution, and desecration of truth revealed in the vision?" Since Daniel's visions encompass the ultimate deliverance of God's people and the establishment of His kingdom, when exactly will that happen? How long until God finally puts down the enemy for good? That's a very important question! It would be a natural question to raise, one that you and I would like to ask if we were at Daniel's side watching the prophetic panorama unfold. The horn power stamps and treads on the saints and sanctuary unmercifully and without any apparent restraint. How long will this go on? How long will all this pain and suffering continue?

As life has continued on our war zone of Planet Earth, "How long?" has been on the minds of God's children for quite some time. It seems that since the Fall the opposition has had the edge, and the "trampling" began in the shadow of Eden with Cain slaying his brother. "How long, O Lord, holy and true, until You judge and avenge our blood" is the cry of those faithful ones slain as martyrs (Rev. 6:10). If this be a legitimate understanding of the intent of the question, we are reminded that the visions of both Daniel 7 and 8 strongly suggest that the enemy has the upper hand, that is, the "trampling" will continue until the "end," until the return of Christ. The grand climax of Daniel's visions goes through to the establishment of God's glorious kingdom. Take note of these reasons why we should understand that the "trampling" will continue to the "end":

1. First of all, Scripture instructs us not to look for the complete fulfillment of these visions till the "end." Daniel 7 takes us to the establishment of God's kingdom (Dan. 7:14, 22, 27). When the angel Gabriel came to explain to Daniel the meaning of the vision of chapter 8, his first words were: "Understand, son of man, that the vision refers to the time of the end" (Dan. 8:17). Next he admonished: "Look, I am making known to you what shall happen in the latter time of the indignation; for at the appointed time the end shall be" (verse 19). His last words to the prophet on this occasion were: "Seal up the vision, for it refers to many days in the future" (verse 26). Any interpretation of these visions that does not reach to the "end," thus culminating in the final setting up of God's kingdom, falls short of the focal point of the prophetic messages.

2. Daniel 7:11 tells us that the pompous horn power meets its end when its body is "destroyed and given to the burning flame" (notice also the phrase "consume and destroy" in verse 26), which Paul interprets as happening at the return of Jesus (2 Thess. 2:8).

The book of Daniel describes the climactic and final end of the horn power as being in contrast to the others before it, who continued a while after having their power taken by another (Dan. 7:12).

3. In Daniel 7:21 and 22 the horn power wages war against the

saints and prevails over them until heaven pronounces judgment in favor of the saints *and* the time comes for them to possess the kingdom, which will not take place until the return of Jesus to this earth (see also verse 26, which pictures the court activity in the first part of the verse, while the final destruction of the horn power we find described in the second part). The first usage of the word "and" in this verse is significant, because the two phrases describe events separated by a period of time, like the "and" in John 5:29, which appears between the resurrection of the righteous and the resurrection of the wicked. The enemy will continue to dominate until the time when the saints possess the kingdom at Jesus' return, an event made possible because prior to that time God has pronounced judgment in their favor. Likewise, in the last chapter of the Bible we see Daniel's "judgment made in favor of the saints" reflected in Jesus' statement: "He who is righteous, let him be righteous still; he who is holy, let him be holy still" (Rev. 22:11). The next verse (which also begins with "and") describes the as yet future coming of Jesus: "And behold, I am coming quickly, and My reward is with Me, to give to every one according to his work" (verse 12).

4. In Daniel 8:25 the horn power persecutes and prospers until it is "broken without hand" (KJV), a phrase that alludes to the coming of Christ, as in the "stone . . . cut out of the mountain without hands" that smites the statue of chapter 2, welcoming in the reign of God's kingdom (Dan. 2:44, 45).

If it is correct that part of the question is "How long will the trampling continue?" and if it is also correct, as the evidence suggests, that the "trampling" continues until Jesus comes back, then we must take into account the fact that it is not God's policy to reveal the exact time of Jesus' return: "But of that day and hour no one knows, not even the angels in heaven, nor the Son, but only the Father" (Mark 13:32).

What happens, then, when we have a question for which no direct answer can be given? In dealing with such an inquiry, we must ask ourselves whether there is any other passage in the Scriptures that we might compare it to. It might be helpful to take a look at Paul's advice to the believers in Thessalonica and see how he reasoned with them. Because they had lost sight of the hope of the resurrection, the apostle reminded them that they would indeed see their departed loved ones again. Christ would raise them at His return (1 Thess. 4:16, 17). When they received this good news, apparently some of the believers understood Paul's letter to mean that Christ's return was imminent, perhaps within days or weeks. As a result, the apostle had to caution them that certain things must take place before Jesus would come back.

Picture yourself in your car with your young child, waiting at the intersection for the light to turn green so that you can continue going straight down the road, and your eager son or daughter demands, "When are we going to be able to go?" You tell them that you don't know that precisely. First, you explain, the cars going across the street have their chance, and then they will get a red light. Next, a green arrow will appear for those cars making left turns in front of you. After that, you will get the green light to go straight. So you tell your child, "I don't know exactly when we'll be able to go, but when you see the green arrow for the left-turners, then you'll know that we're getting very close." The answer you give is not direct, but nonetheless helpful.

In a similar way, Paul drew from the prophecies of Daniel and skillfully instructed his Thessalonian readers that certain things must happen before Christ's advent and their reunion with their loved ones. Paul well knew that Rome, the power that wielded the scepter in his day, was the fourth kingdom, the indescribable beast of Daniel's prophecy. It would be followed by a great falling away and the rise of the boastful and arrogant "lawless one" (NIV) or "man of sin," the apostle's expression for the horn power, whose destruction would coincide with the return of Jesus (see 2 Thess. 2:1-8). But as long as civil Rome was in power, Paul knew that the coming of Jesus, according to prophecy, could not yet take place.

"And now you know what is restraining, that he [the lawless one] may be revealed in his own time. For the mystery of lawlessness is already at work; only he who now restrains [civil Rome] will do so until he is taken out of the way. And then the lawless one will be revealed, whom the Lord will consume with the breath of His mouth and destroy with the brightness of His coming" (verses 6-8).

Paul was arguing that when Rome would fall and give place to the great apostasy, the horn power, then Christ's coming would be closer, for the horn power's destruction would take place at His coming.

Thus we see that the Epistle writer did not give a direct answer to his friends in Thessalonica as to when Jesus would return, because that was not possible. Instead, he acquainted them with the sequence of events that must occur prior to the Advent, thus encouraging them to be patient and wise in their hope of the Second Coming.

Likewise, a few days after Jesus' resurrection, His disciples eagerly asked Him an important question: "Therefore, when they had come together, they asked Him, saying, 'Lord, will You at this time restore the kingdom to Israel?' And He said to them, 'It is not for you to know times or seasons which the Father has put in His own authority. But you shall receive power when the Holy Spirit has come upon you; and you shall be witnesses to Me in Jerusalem, and in all Judea and Samaria, and to the end of the earth'" (Acts 1:6-8).

In the context of all that had happened in the previous few weeks, climaxed by Christ's victorious and glorious resurrection, we can well appreciate the enthusiasm their question conveyed. But notice that Jesus did not answer their inquiry directly. Instead, He pointed their attention to something of critical importance: specifically, the outpouring of the Holy Spirit, which would enable them to be effective witnesses. That had to take place before the event that was the subject of their question. Although Jesus did not answer the question exactly the way they might have hoped, He opened their eyes to something vital that must be fulfilled before the restoration of the kingdom could become reality.

Looking again at the question of Daniel 8:13, and viewing it from this perspective, what can we learn? If the horn's capacity to persecute will be completely terminated only at Christ's second coming, and if it is also true that it is not God's will to pinpoint the date of that event, can we determine at all how long the "trampling" and abuse of God's children will go on? We would not expect an answer that would specify the day of Jesus' return, because God in His wisdom has chosen not to reveal that.

On the other hand, if it is also true that the conclusion of God's final review, the pre-Advent judgment, must be achieved before He returns with His reward, an event that the vision of chapter 7 highlights so vividly, and if the exact time of Jesus' return is not to be disclosed, at least the date when heaven's court will convene would be of encouragement and help, because that is something that must also end before the "trampling" forever stops. The "numbering" of its kingdom must be finalized before the domination of wickedness will cease. The "weighing" must be completed before evil is overthrown. Daniel's prophecy is telling us that exactly how long the "trampling" will continue is not to be revealed, but that we can know the date for the sitting of heaven's tribunal, which must finish its work before the saints possess the kingdom. Those who become aware of it can then sense where we are in prophecy's timeline.

Although the question posed in Daniel 8:13 does not explicitly include the phrase "he cast truth down to the ground" (verse 12), since that was a prominent part of the horn's destructive activity, it might not be inappropriate to ask the question, How does the investigative judgment bring about the end of truth being cast to the ground?

The horn power, in its pagan Rome phase, "cast truth to the ground" in the *person* of God, by nailing Jesus, who is the "way, the truth, and the life" (John 14:6), to a cross. Jesus is the embodiment of truth. He is the "Amen" (the Hebrew root for the word "truth"; see also Revelation 3:14). Jesus came to earth to reveal the truth about God, the truth about His character of love, to remove the smudges placed against the divine reputation by the character assassin Satan.

But the intent of the question looked forward not just to when Jesus lived here on earth but also to a later event, the investigative judgment, as restoring what the horn power had destroyed. The horn power in its papal phase "cast truth to the ground" by introducing numerous false doctrines that have had the effect of tarnishing the *reputation* of God, of saying something untrue about His character. A "doctrine" is not just a statement of religious fact. It is essentially a statement about God and His character. Thus, a false teaching misleads us in our understanding and appreciation of His character and person. For example, the teaching that God commits those who reject Him to a never-ending hell that punishes sinners for eternity says something untrue about His character and smudges His reputation. The truth that the Bible brings to light never stands as an independent thing, but is always a truth *about God.*

How long will the truth about God be dragged in the mud and His reputation stained? Part of the restoration toward which this prophecy looks is the reinstatement of certain truths about God that the horn power has "cast to the ground." The Seventh-day Adventist Church, called into being at the time that this longest time prophecy culminates, has been commissioned to reintroduce to the Christian church those truths about God that the horn power had removed, defaced, or replaced by other doctrines not found in His Word.

In what other way does the investigative judgment accomplish this restoration of God's reputation? As we have seen, this last-day judicial review pronounces judgment in favor of the saints and exonerates their records through God's grace. Their surrendered lives—living in harmony with His law—testifies to the proposition that God does not require too much, that He is not the tyrant that the devil has made Him out to be, and that His grace is sufficient to save anyone who comes to Him. At the same time they vindicate God's name and uplift His truth.

So we see that verse 14 of Daniel 8 acts as a direct answer to the implicit question "How long will truth be cast down?" because at the end of the 2300-day/year prophecy a movement began that restored truths about God which had been lost or replaced. Thus, the investigative judgment restores God's reputation. We also see that verse 14 is an indirect answer to the explicit question "How long will the trampling go on?" in that the conclusion of the investigative judgment is a necessary prerequisite to Christ's return, when the horn power will be destroyed.

Chapter Seven

Christ's Entrance
Into the Most Holy Place

Some have objected that to teach that Christ waited until 1844 to enter the Most Holy Place of heaven's sanctuary is not defensible, since the Bible states that He has been at the right hand of the Father since His ascension, a fact supported by the dying vision of the martyr Stephen.

But to say that Christ did not enter the Most Holy Place of the sanctuary in heaven for the purpose of beginning the investigative judgment until 1844 does not have to mean that He was not in the presence of His Father before that time, or even that He was not in the Most Holy Place prior to 1844. It simply indicates that He began a new phase of His ministry at that time.

We have in our language many phrases that use geographical imagery to convey function. For example, we know the difference between saying a judge is "on the bench" and saying an athlete is "on the bench." And we know what it means when a broker asks if we're "in the market" or someone says they're "at a crossroads." It is reasonable to allow language, particularly in the sanctuary context of types and symbols, to perform this same function and be seen in this light. We can understand the entering of Jesus into the Most Holy Place as the beginning of a new phase of His ministry. Nothing requires us to make "He entered the Most Holy Place in 1844" and "He was in the presence of His Father upon His ascension" mutually exclusive.

Let's also not forget that the types contained in the Day of Atonement service span widely across the timeline of our world's history. At a bare minimum, Yom Kippur includes events from the cross to the millennium, with the slaying of the Lord's goat representing Calvary, and the leading away of Azazel (the scapegoat) pointing toward the 1,000 years following His second coming. In addition, on the Day of Atonement the high priest went into the Most Holy Place not merely one time, but multiple times.

Adventists should have no problem acknowledging that Jesus entered the presence of His Father prior to 1844. But neither should they be castigated for believing that Yom Kippur held a special judicial significance, that the end product of the day's service was to seal the believer's destiny, and that this aspect foreshadowed that part of the judgment—the investigative phase—that other scriptures declare takes place prior to Jesus' return.

Chapter Eight

Conclusion

Repeatedly Scripture has presented a picture of a deity condescending to speak our language so that we can be at ease with the decisions He makes and the judgments He pronounces. Consistently we find Him *investigating before He takes action.* If God investigated before He took action in these stories and examples, how much more would we expect Him to do so at the time of the end of the world, when the grand climax of all things will come to pass!

We have seen within the biblical teaching of the judgment that one phase of it, an investigative aspect, takes place prior to Jesus' return. Both prophecy and narrative clearly teach it. The concept is also rooted in the word "cleansed" used in Daniel 8:14 and is consistent with the character of a God who more than anything else wants His creatures to be comfortable with those decisions that will finalize the destinies of earth's inhabitants.

In the visions of Daniel 7 and 8 the investigative judgment is the pivotal point that shifts the momentum from wickedness's dominating to righteousness's reigning. It is not that the saints possess the kingdom immediately upon the favorable verdict rendered in the court scene—just as a period of time occurred between the shutting of Noah's ark and onset of the Flood—but that God has recognized as final the decision that each individual has made about Him.

Allow me to express my personal testimony about having looked into this teaching. This study has been an immeasurable blessing to me in that it has given me greater confidence in a concept fundamental to our church's theological position. As I have examined the doctrine I have concluded that it accurately reflects the teaching of Scripture and that it requires no outside assistance whatsoever to justify its existence. Others may question whether the teaching is biblical, but my mind is at rest. The Bible, and the Bible alone, is sufficient to establish the pre-Advent judgment. Now, when questions or accusations rise regarding its validity, I can affirm the teaching with even greater assurance. I have examined the watch and found it to be a Rolex!

We might ask the question, If this takes place in heaven while humans are on earth and not there personally, and God already knows who is to be saved or lost, then for whose benefit does He conduct the pre-Advent judgment? We know that during the millennium God will allow the redeemed access to the books of record so that they can have every question answered. Revelation 20:4 states: "And I saw thrones, and they sat on them, and judgment was committed to them." (The Greek word for "judgment" here is *krima,* which has the implication of *"result* of judgment," in contrast to the more frequently used *krisis,* which has the connotation of *"process* of judgment." The saints receive the "results" of the judgment to review and satisfy any inquiries they might have.)

And let us not forget that the angels and the inhabitants of worlds not infected by the virus of sin will be receiving new neighbors in the hereafter. Though possessing greater abilities than members of the human race, they are not omniscient, as is God. They do not have the ability to read hearts, minds, and motives, as does the Ancient of Days. Therefore, prior to Christ's coming, this phase of the judgment takes place so that Jesus can have His reward with Him when He returns, and so that all creatures throughout His far-flung universe can rest in absolute confidence that those whom He is bringing to heaven are "safe to save."

Openness begets confidence. From the wings of the operating room the universe has been watching God perform surgery on the patient Earth, afflicted with the cancer of sin. When God first detected the virus long ago in heaven, He could have quietly euthanatized Lucifer and his followers. But this approach He didn't take.

Rather, He allowed the disease to develop fully so that all could see its ugly and lethal nature. God had every right to exterminate the rebels instantly, but He did not. He chose to use the "open" approach at sin's inception, and He has chosen to employ the same at its conclusion, by making available to angels and the other unfallen creatures, prior to His return, the records of those decisions of the human heart that only God can read.

Sin is not so much an act as it is a condition. It is true that the Bible speaks often of the "acts" of sin, but iniquity is much deeper than outward behavior. While deeds evidence the existence of sin, it originates in the thoughts. It exhibits its symptoms in the "hand," but is an ailment of the "heart." As such, only God can read the heart and know its true standing. Not even angels can read the thoughts and weigh the motives of the mind.

The investigative judgment opens the records so that God's creatures who remained faithful to Him can see what He sees, can know what He knows, and can thus have complete confidence that those He is bringing home are forever free of the virus of sin. Could God simply say to them: "These are all OK to bring to heaven. You'll have to trust Me on that"? Yes, He could—but He doesn't. He prefers an open approach.

Suppose a doctor who works at an orphanage proposes to adopt and bring home an orphan who had previously been sick with a dangerous and contagious disease. The doctor could tell his family, "I've tested Bobby, and he's fine. He's not bringing the germs with him when he comes to live here. Our family won't be in any danger. You'll have to believe me that I've checked him on the inside and that he's free of disease." Now, the children of the doctor, who had seen Bobby when they visited Dad at work, had observed the blotches on Bobby's skin that indicated his disease. Yes, it's true that on the outside he now looks well. But is the disease still on the inside? they wonder. And so, because bringing Bobby home to live with them is such a life-changing event, and because he wants his family to be at ease, the doctor first takes home the blood tests and other exams that demonstrate to his family what they otherwise couldn't see—that Bobby's OK on the inside, too, and that their home will still be safe if he comes to live with them.

And because sin is a condition of the heart that only God can read, He graciously goes the second mile and does something He isn't required to do. He makes available to His heavenly creatures the "test results," the investigative judgment, so that they can see and know that their home will be safe from another outbreak of sin when God brings those He has healed to heaven.

For us on earth, what is the significance of believing that there is to be a pre-Advent judgment, and that we are now living during its time of operation? First, no matter what else, if God takes the time and trouble to provide information regarding His plans and methods of doing things, I would be shortchanging myself by refusing to accept and believe it, for any truth is a part of the greater whole, without which the whole would not be complete.

Second, let's not forget another important point: along with all the other spectacularly fulfilled signs of Bible prophecy, obviously an understanding of the pre-Advent judgment plants an extremely significant marker on the timeline of earth's history. Realizing that we now live in the time when the "hour of His judgment has come" (Rev. 14:6, 7) adds clarity, conviction, urgency, and solemnity to the proclamation of the gospel. It is not business as usual in the unfolding of salvation's story—God is ready to wrap things up. To use sports parlance, we're in the fourth quarter now, and the two-minute warning has sounded.

Third, God gave us this information for a reason. Though we are not personally present when the heavenly courtroom conducts its business, it should inspire and encourage us to know that such a judicial review exists and that it reflects absolute justice as well as divine mercy within the context of redeeming love. A Savior named Jesus serves as Judge and Advocate.

Suppose you wanted to attend an institution of higher learning but couldn't afford its tuition. Then you learned that a scholarship was available, made possible by a generous donor. So you submitted your name and applied for the award. Wouldn't you be interested to know that first of all a selection committee would be making the decision as to who would receive the scholarship and that it wouldn't be awarded on the basis of some arbitrary thing such as flipping a coin? And though you wouldn't be personally present when they met, wouldn't you appreciate the fact that those on the decision board came from a background similar to yours and had empathy for your situation? Wouldn't it inspire you to know that the process that governed the life-changing decision they were to make was based on fairness and was without prejudice? And as the school year approached, without question you would want to know when the result of that decision would be made final—if not the exact date of their decision, at least when the committee would begin its selection process. Most certainly you would have the keenest interest in all of these things! God in His love and wisdom has revealed all of this to us when Scripture speaks about the investigative judgment.

The most important benefit of understanding God's system of justice is not the proving of the technical accuracy of a Bible teaching. It is not the appreciating of the Bible's impressive logic and linguistics. It is the emerging of a picture. This picture is not about dates, charts, or timetables. Rather, it is the portrait of God that comes into view through this study. Or perhaps I should say the "collage" of God, for it really is a picture composed of many images.

The theme of the picture is the character of God, a God whose reputation has been smeared by Satan's conspiracy. It is the portrait of a God who is willing to do anything He can think of to win the confidence and trust of His lost children. He could have proclaimed, "This is the way it is. This one is saved and this one is lost. I am God—it's for Me to decide and for you to accept." But that's not His way of doing things. It's not who He is. Rather, in the revealed Word we see a picture of a God willing to lower Himself to an incredible level to speak a language His creatures can understand. We see here the picture of a "second mile" God willing to go far beyond the mere requirement of divine justice to cultivate in us an appreciation for His fairness in the decisions that affect us. He is omniscient, but He will conduct Himself in a way that His creatures will comprehend, by *investigating before taking action.*

The question comes to mind: If there were a truth revealed by the Bible calculated to challenge us to get ready for Christ's soon return by informing us that we're now living in the "hour of His judgment," and to cultivate within us confidence and appreciation concerning His fair and just administration, who would gain the most by undermining such a teaching, by obscuring such a picture? This is a message that needs to be heralded, not hushed; proclaimed, not disclaimed!

In this collage we find a snapshot of the Eden-walking Creator inquiring of Adam and Eve in the cool of the day before pronouncing the first curses. There is a clip of Him questioning Cain before he is marked. We see a photo of Him looking into the wickedness of Noah's day, and one of God coming down to observe the rebellion at Babel. A travel-worn Stranger converses with His friend Abraham, and the two messengers investigate Sodom and Gomorrah before the cities' destruction. There is the print of His angel flying above Egypt, looking for the blood on the doorposts. A portion of this collage shows flaming letters appearing on a wall in a soon-to-be doomed Babylonian banquet hall, indicating that the kingdom's account has been double-checked and weighed. The collage includes the scene of a "stooping" Jesus, writing the sins of His enemies in the dust of the Temple pavement.

These pictures testify of a God of supreme love, not willing that any should perish, reluctant to dispense punishment, and doing so only when every other avenue has been exhausted. He acts only after personally checking into each case so as to render the appropriate and just reward.

A part of the collage, right in the middle, is reserved as open space for right now, because it is for a scene yet to be developed. That panorama will take its rightful place as centerpiece of the collage, bringing it to its completion, when the saints gather on the glassy sea and raise their collective voices in the anthem, "Great and marvelous are Your works, Lord God Almighty! Just and true are Your ways, O King of the saints!" (Rev. 15:3).

Forever put to rest will be the charges brought by Satan. And forever dispelled will be the insinuations of the character assassin.

Throughout His vast universe His creatures will be eternally secure and serene in the confidence that He has done all things well, that He is worthy of their trust and entitled to their worship. His reputation stands everlastingly vindicated, with all tarnish and smudges erased, and peace will reign forever. May that day come quickly!